FIRST THINGS FIRST Students' Book

An Integrated Course for Beginners

By the same author

Sixty Steps to Précis
Poetry and Prose Appreciation
Essay and Letter-writing
A First Book in Comprehension, Précis and Composition
The Carters of Greenwood *(Cineloops)*
Detectives from Scotland Yard *(Longman Structural Readers, Stage 1)*
Car Thieves *(Longman Structural Readers, Stage 1)*
Worth A Fortune *(Longman Structural Readers, Stage 2)*
April Fools' Day *(Longman Structural Readers, Stage 2)*
Operation Mastermind *(Longman Structural Readers, Stage 3)*
Professor Boffin's Umbrella *(Longman Structural Readers, Stage 2)*
Question and Answer: Graded Aural/Oral Exercises
For and Against
Reading and Writing English. A First Year Programme for Children
Look, Listen and Learn! Sets 1–4 An Integrated Course for Children

NEW CONCEPT ENGLISH
Uniform with this Volume:
Practice and Progress: An Integrated Course for Pre-Intermediate Students
Developing Skills: An Integrated Course for Intermediate Students
Fluency in English: An Integrated Course for Advanced Students

NEW CONCEPT ENGLISH *in two Volume edition*
First Things First Part 1–2
Practice and Progress Part 1–2

NEW CONCEPT ENGLISH

FIRST THINGS FIRST Students' Book
An Integrated Course for Beginners

L. G. ALEXANDER

Illustrated by Tom Bailey and Ted Pettengell

LONGMAN

LONGMAN GROUP LIMITED
London

Associated companies, branches and representatives
throughout the world

First published 1967
Twenty Second impression 1976

ISBN 0 582 52329 X

Please note that minor editorial changes have been
made in this impression following suggestions
received from teachers and students in various parts
of the world.

Printed in England by Benham & Co. Ltd,
Sheepen Road, Colchester, Essex CO3 3LH

CONTENTS

Lesson 1

Excúse me!

Yés?

Ís thís yóur hándbag?

Párdon?

Ís thís yóur hándbag?

Yés, it ís.

Thánk you véry múch.

Lesson 2 Is this your . . . ?

Exercise

Copy this:

Excuse me. Is this your handbag?
Yes, it is. Thank you very much.

Lesson 3

My cóat and my umbrélla pléase.

Hére is my tícket.

Thánk you, sír.
Númber fíve.

Hére is your umbrélla
and your cóat.

Thís is nót mý umbrélla.
Sórry, sír.

Is thís your umbrélla?
Nó, it ísn't!

Is thís it?
Yés, it ís.
Thánk you véry múch.

Lesson 4   Is this your . . . ?

1
Is this your pen?

2
Is this your pencil?

3
Is this your book?

4
Is this your watch?

5
Is this your coat?

6
Is this your dress?

7
Is this your skirt?

8
Is this your shirt?

9
Is this your car?

10
Is this your house?

11
Is this your suit?

12
Is this your school?

13
Is this your teacher?

14
Is this your son?

15
Is this your daughter?

Exercise

Copy this:

This is not my umbrella.
Sorry, sir.
Is this your umbrella?
No, it isn't!

MR BLAKE: Góod mórning.
STUDENTS: Góod mórning, Mr Bláke.

MR BLAKE: Thís is Míss Álice Dupónt.
Álice is a néw stúdent.
She is Frénch.

MR BLAKE: Álice, thís is Háns.
He is Gérman.
HANS: Hów do you dó?

MR BLAKE: And thís is Brítt.
She is Swédish.
BRITT: Hów do you dó?

MR BLAKE: And thís is Dimítri.
He is Gréek.
DIMITRI: Hów do you dó?

MR BLAKE: And thís is Pául.
He's Brazílian.
PAUL: Hów do you dó?

MR BLAKE: And thís is Stélla.
She's Spánish.
STELLA: Hów do you dó?

Lesson 6 What make is it?

8

It's a Volvo. (Swedish)

9

It's a Citroen. (French)

10

It's a Volkswagen. (German)

11

It's a Daf. (Dutch)

12

It's a Moskovitch. (Russian)

13

It's a Morris. (English)

14

It's a Buick. (American)

15

It's a Fiat. (Italian)

Exercise

Look at this:

> Stella is a student. ---- isn't German. ---- is Spanish.
> Stella is a student. She isn't German. She is Spanish.

Copy this. Put in: He, She *or* It.

Alice is a student. ---- isn't German. ---- is French.
This is her car. ---- is a French car.
Hans is a student. ---- isn't French. ---- is German.
This is his car. ---- is a German car.

ROBERT: I am a néw stúdent.
My náme's Róbert.
ALICE: Hów do you dó?
My náme's Álice.

ROBERT: Áre you Frénch?
ALICE: Yés, I ám.

ALICE: Are yóu French, tóo?
ROBERT: Nó, I am nót.

ALICE: Whát nationálity áre you?
ROBERT: I'm Itálian.

ROBERT: Áre you a téacher?
ALICE: Nó, I'm nót.

ROBERT: Whát's your jób?
ALICE: I'm a týpist.

ALICE: Whát's yóur job?
ROBERT: Í'm an enginéer.

Lesson 8 What's your job?

11

I'm a policeman.

12

I'm a policewoman.

13

I'm a taxi-driver.

14

I'm an air-hostess.

15

I'm a postman.

16

I'm a nurse.

17

I'm a mechanic.

18

I'm a barber.

19

I'm a housewife.

20

I'm a milkman.

Exercise

Look at this:

> My name ---- Stella. I ---- Spanish.
> My name is Stella. I am Spanish.

Copy this. Put in am *or* is.

My name ---- Robert. I ---- a student. I ---- Italian.
Alice ---- not Italian. She ---- French.
Mr Blake ---- my teacher. He ---- not French.

Lesson 9

MR FORD: Góod afternóon, Mrs Dávis.
MRS DAVIS: Góod afternóon, Mr Fórd.

MR FORD: Hów are yóu todáy?
MRS DAVIS: I'm véry wéll, thánk you.
And yóu?

MR FORD: I'm fíne, thánks.

MR FORD: Hów is Mŕ Dávis?
MRS DAVIS: He's fíne, thánks.
Hów is Mŕs Fórd?
MR FORD: She's véry wéll, tóo, Mrs Dávis.

MR FORD: Góodbye, Mrs Dávis.
Níce to sée you.
MRS DAVIS: Níce to sée yóu, tóo, Mr Fórd.
Góodbye.

Lesson 10 Look at . . .

11
that man!
(fat)

12
that woman!
(thin)

13
that policeman!
(tall)

14
that policewoman!
(short)

15
that mechanic!
(dirty)

16
that nurse!
(clean)

17
Mr Ford!
(hot)

18
Mrs Ford!
(cold)

19
that milkman!
(old)

20
that air-hostess!
(young)

21
that barber!
(busy)

22
that housewife!
(lazy)

Exercise
Look at this:

Robert isn't a teacher. ---- an engineer.
Robert isn't a teacher. He's an engineer.

Copy this. Put in He's , She's *or* It's .

Mr Blake isn't a student. ---- a teacher.
This isn't my umbrella. ---- your umbrella.
Alice isn't a teacher. ---- a typist.
Mr Ford isn't cold. ---- hot.
Stella isn't Brazilian. ---- Spanish.
This isn't a German car. ---- a Swedish car.

Lesson 11

TEACHER: Whóse shírt is thát?

TEACHER: Is thís yóur shírt, Fránk?
FRANK: Nó, sír.
It's nót mý shírt.

FRANK: Thís is mý shírt.
Mý shírt is blúe.

TEACHER: Is thís shírt Tím's?
FRANK: Perháps it ís, sír.
Tím's shírt is whíte.

TEACHER: Tím!
TIM: Yés, sír?

TEACHER: Is thís yóur shírt?
TIM: Yés, sir.

TEACHER: Hére you are.
Cátch!
TIM: Thánk you, sír.

Lesson 12   Whose is this . . ? This is my/your/his/her . .
Whose is that . . .? That is my/your/his/her . .

22

handbag
It is Stella's.

23

car
It is Paul's.

24

coat
It is Miss Dupont's.

25

umbrella
It is Mr Ford's.

26

pen
It is my son's.

27

dress
It is my daughter's.

28

suit
It's my father's.

29

skirt
It's my mother's.

30

blouse
It's my sister's.

31

tie
It's my brother's.

Exercise
Look at this:

> Hans is here. That is ---- car.
> Hans is here. That is his car.

Copy this. Put in my, your, his *or* her.

Stella is here. That is ---- car.
Excuse me, Mr Ford. Is this ---- umbrella?
I am an air-hostess. ---- name is Britt.
Paul is here, too. That is ---- coat.

MRS BROWN: Whát cólour's your néw dréss?
MRS WHITE: It's gréen.

MRS WHITE: Cóme upstáirs and sée it.
MRS BROWN: Thánk you.

MRS WHITE: Lóok!
Hére it ís!
MRS BROWN: Thát's a níce dréss.
It's véry smárt.

MRS WHITE: My hát's néw, tóo.
MRS BROWN: Whát cólour is it?

MRS WHITE: It's the sáme cólour.
It's gréen, tóo.

MRS BROWN: That *is* a lóvely hát!

Lesson **14**　What colour's your . . . ?

20

umbrella

30

car

40

shirt

50

coat

60

case

70

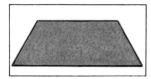

carpet

80

blouse

90

tie

100

hat

101

dog

Exercise

Look at this:

> This is Stella. This is her handbag.
> *This is Stella's handbag.*

Join in the same way:
This is Paul. This is his car.
This is Miss Dupont. This is her coat.
This is Mrs Davis. This is her dog.
This is my father. This is his suit.
This is my daughter. This is her dress.

Lesson **15**

CUSTOMS OFFICER: Áre you Swédish?
GIRLS: Nó, we are nót.
We are Dánish.

CUSTOMS OFFICER: Áre your fríends Dánish, tóo?
GIRLS: Nó, they are nót.
They are Norwégian.

CUSTOMS OFFICER: Your pássports pléase.
GIRLS: Hére they áre.

CUSTOMS OFFICER: Áre thése yóur cáses?
GIRLS: Nó, they áren't.

GIRLS: Óur cáses are brówn.
Hére they áre.

CUSTOMS OFFICER: Áre you tóurists?
GIRLS: Yés, we áre.

CUSTOMS OFFICER: Áre your fríends tóurists tóo?
GIRLS: Yés, they áre.

CUSTOMS OFFICER: Thát's fíne.
Thánk you véry múch.

Lesson 16

Are you . . .

20
Russian?

30
English?

40
American?

50
Dutch?

Are these your . . . ?   What colour are your . . . ?

60
red books

70
white shirts

80
grey coats

90
yellow tickets

100
blue suits

101
black and grey hats

102
green passports

103
black umbrellas

104
white handbags

105
orange ties

106
brown and white dogs

107
blue pens

108
red cars

109
green dresses

110
yellow blouses

Exercise

Look at this:

| It is . . . Swedish car. | *It is a Swedish car.* |
| She is . . . air-hostess. | *She is an air-hostess.* |

Copy this. Put in *a* or *an*.
It is . . . English car.
It is . . . Russian car.
It is . . . Italian car.
It is . . . French car.
It is . . . American car.
Robert is not . . . teacher.
He is . . . engineer.

Lesson **17**

MR JACKSON: Cóme and méet
our employées, Mr Ríchards.
MR RICHARDS: Thánk you, Mr Jáckson.

MR JACKSON: Thís is Míss Gréy
and thís is Míss Táylor.
MR RICHARDS: Hów do you dó?

MR RICHARDS: Thóse gírls are véry prétty.
Whát are their jóbs?
MR JACKSON: They're týpists.

MR JACKSON: Thís is Mŕ Báker
and thís is Mŕ Shórt.
MR RICHARDS: Hów do you dó?

MR RICHARDS: Théy aren't véry búsy!
Whát are their jóbs?
MR JACKSON: They're clérks.
They're véry lázy.

MR RICHARDS: Whó is thís yóung mán?
MR JACKSON: Thís is Jím.
Hé's our óffice bóy!

Lesson **18**   What are their jobs?

100 clerks

200 typists

300 mechanics

400 engineers

500 barbers

600 teachers

700 customs officers

800 taxi-drivers

900 nurses

1000 air-hostesses

1001 housewives

1002 milkmen

1003 postmen

1004 policemen

1005 policewomen

Exercise

Look at this:

> Those men are lazy.   . . . are clerks.
> *Those men are lazy. They are clerks.*

Copy this. Put in He, She, We or They.
That man is tall.   . . . is a policeman.
Those girls are busy.   . . . are typists.
Our names are Britt and Inge.   . . . are Swedish.
Look at our office boy.   . . . is very busy.
Look at Miss Grey.   . . . is very pretty.
Mr Baker and Mr Short are employees.   . . . are clerks.

Lesson **19**

MOTHER:	Whát's the mátter, chíldren?
GIRL:	We're tíred . . .
BOY:	. . . and thírsty, mum.

MOTHER:	Sít down hére.

MOTHER:	Áre you áll ríght nów?
BOY:	Nó, we áren't.

MOTHER:	Lóok!
	Thére's an íce-créam mán.

MOTHER:	Twó íce-créams pléase.

MOTHER:	Hére you áre, chíldren.
CHILDREN:	Thánks, mum.

GIRL:	Thése íce-créams are níce.

MOTHER:	Áre you áll ríght nów?
CHILDREN:	Yés, we áre, thánk you!

Lesson **20**   Look at them!

105

They're clean.

106

They're dirty.

217

They're hot.

218

They're cold.

321

They're fat.

322

They're thin.

433

They're big.

434

They're small.

545
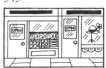
They're open.

546

They're shut.

657

They're light.

658

They're heavy.

769

They're old.

770

They're young.

881

They're old.

882

They're new.

998

They're short.

999

They're tall.

1000

They're short.

1001

They're long

Exercise

Look at this:

> Those children . . . thirsty.
> *Those children are thirsty.*

Copy this. Put in am , is or are .
Those children . . . tired.
Their mother . . . tired, too.
That ice-cream man . . . very busy.
His ice-creams . . . very nice.
What's the matter, children? We . . . thirsty.
What's the matter, Tim? I . . . tired.

MAN: Gíve me a bóok pléase, Jáne.

WOMAN: Whích bóok?

WOMAN: Thís one?

MAN: Nó, nót thát one.
         The réd one.

WOMAN: Thís one?
MAN: Yés, pléase.

WOMAN: Hére you áre.
MAN: Thánk you.

Lesson 22 Give me/him/her/us/them a . . .
Which one?

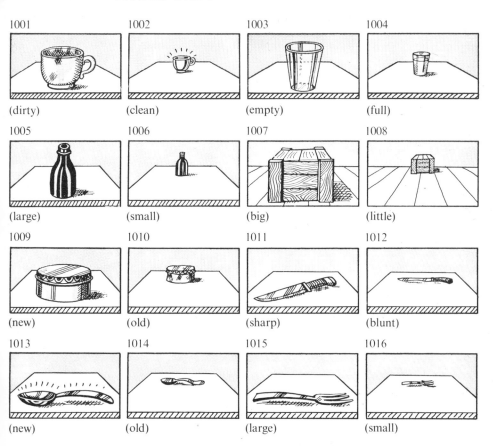

1001 (dirty)	1002 (clean)	1003 (empty)	1004 (full)
1005 (large)	1006 (small)	1007 (big)	1008 (little)
1009 (new)	1010 (old)	1011 (sharp)	1012 (blunt)
1013 (new)	1014 (old)	1015 (large)	1016 (small)

Exercise
Look at this:

Is this Tim's shirt? No, it's not. . . . shirt is white.
Is this Tim's shirt? No, it's not. His shirt is white.

Copy this. Put in His, Her, Our *or* Their
Is this Miss Grey's coat? No, it's not. . . . coat is grey.
Are these your pens? No, they're not. . . . pens are blue.
Is this Mr Jackson's hat? No, it's not. . . . hat is black.
Are these the children's books? No, they're not. . . . books are red.
Is this Mrs Davis's dog? No, it's not. . . . dog is brown and white.
Is this your father's tie? No, it's not. . . . tie is orange.

22

Lesson 23

MAN: Gíve me some glásses pléase, Jáne

WOMAN: Whích glásses?

WOMAN: Thése glásses?

MAN: Nó, nót thóse.
The ónes on the shélf.

WOMAN: Thése?
MAN: Yés, pléase.

WOMAN: Hére you áre.
MAN: Thánks.

Lesson 24 Give me/him/her/us/them some . . .
Which ones?

1117

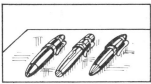

pens/on the desk

1218

ties/on the chair

1319

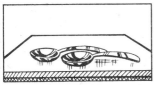

spoons/on the table

1420

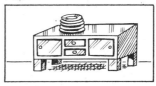

plates/on the sideboard

1521

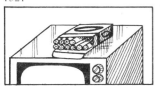

cigarettes/on the television

1622

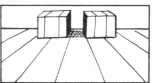

boxes/on the floor

1723

bottles/on the dressing-table

1824

books/on the shelf

1925

magazines/on the bed

2000

newspapers/on the radio

Exercise
Look at this:

> Give Tim this shirt. Give . . . this one, too.
> *Give Tim this shirt. Give him this one, too.*

Copy this. Put in me, him, her, us, *or* them.

Give Jane this watch. Give . . . this one, too.
Give the children these ice-creams. Give . . . these ones, too.
Give Tom this book. Give , . . this one, too.
That is my passport. Give . . . my passport please.
That is my coat. Give . . . my coat please.
Those are our umbrellas. Give . . . our umbrellas please.

Mŕs Smíth's kítchen is smáll.
There is a refrígerator in the kítchen.
The refrígerator is whíte.
It is ón the ríght.
There is an eléctric cóoker in the kítchen.
The cóoker is blúe.
It is ón the léft.
There is a táble
in the míddle of the róom.
There is a bóttle on the táble.
The bóttle is émpty.
There is a cúp on the táble, tóo.
The cúp is cléan.

Lesson 26   Where is it?

3000
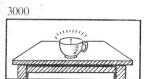
There is a cup on the table.
The cup is clean.

4000
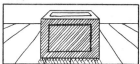
There is a box on the floor.
The box is large.

5000
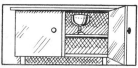
There is a glass in the
sideboard.
The glass is empty.

6000
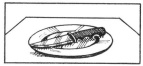
There is a knife on the plate.
The knife is sharp.

7000

There is a fork on the tin.
The fork is dirty.

8000
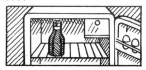
There is a bottle in the
refrigerator.
The bottle is full.

9000
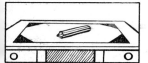
There is a pencil on the desk.
The pencil is blunt.

10,000

There is a spoon in the cup.
The spoon is small.

Exercise
Look at this:

> Give me . . . book. Which book? . . . book on the table.
> *Give me a book. Which book? The book on the table.*

Copy these. Put in a *or* the.
Give me . . . glass. Which glass? . . . empty one.
Give me some cups. Which cups? . . . cups on the table.
Is there . . . book on . . . table? Yes, there is. Is . . . book red?
Is there . . . knife in that box? Yes, there is. Is . . . knife sharp?

Mŕs Smíth's líving-róom is lárge.
There is a télevision in the róom.
The télevision is néar the wíndow.
There are some mágazínes on the télevision.
There is a táble in the róom.
There are some néwspapers on the táble.
There are some ármchairs in the róom.
The ármchairs are néar the táble.
There is a rádio in the róom.
The rádio is néar the dóor.
There are some bóoks on the rádio.
There are some píctures in the róom.
The píctures are ón the wáll.

Lesson **28**   Where are they?

1120

There are some cigarettes
on the dressing-table.
They are near that box.

3340

There are some trousers
on the bed.
They are near that shirt.

5560

There are some shoes on the floor.
They're near the bed.

7780

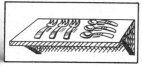

There are some forks on the shelf.
They're near those spoons.

9999

There are some tickets on the shelf.
They're in that handbag.

2230

There are some plates on the
cooker.
They are clean.

4450

There are some bottles in the
refrigerator.
They are empty.

6670

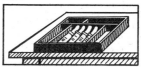

There are some knives on the table.
They're in that box.

8890

There are some bottles on the sideboard.
They're near those tins.

10,001

There are some glasses on the radio.
They're near those bottles.

Exercise

Look at these:

a book – some books; a man – some men; a housewife – some housewives.

Now look at this:

There *is a book* on the desk.   *There are some books on the desk.*

Copy these and change in the same way:
There *is a pencil* on the desk.
There *is a knife* near that tin.

There *is a policeman* in the kitchen.
There *is a newspaper* in the living-room.
There *is a typist* in the office.

Lesson **29**

Mrs Jones: Cóme in, Béssie.

Mrs Jones: Shút the dóor pléase.

Mrs Jones: Thís bédroom's véry untídy.
Bessie: Whát must I dó, Mrs Jónes?

Mrs Jones: Ópen the wíndow
and áir the róom.

Mrs Jones: Then pút thése clóthes
in the wárdrobe.

Mrs Jones: Then máke the béd.

Mrs Jones: Dúst the dréssing-táble.

Mrs Jones: Then swéep the flóor.

Lesson **30**   What must I do?

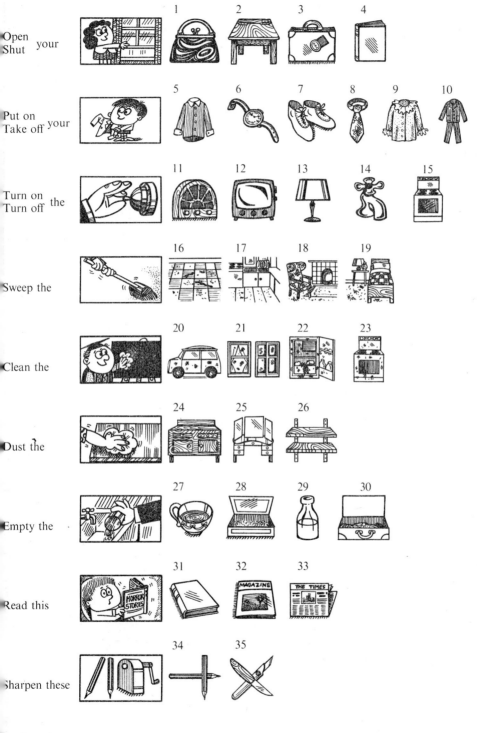

Open / Shut your 1 2 3 4

Put on / Take off your 5 6 7 8 9 10

Turn on / Turn off the 11 12 13 14 15

Sweep the 16 17 18 19

Clean the 20 21 22 23

Dust the 24 25 26

Empty the 27 28 29 30

Read this 31 32 33

Sharpen these 34 35

Look at this:

The cup isn't empty. *Empty it!*

Change in the same way:
The window isn't clean.
The door isn't shut.
The wardrobe isn't open.

30

JEAN: Whére's Sálly, Jáck?
JACK: She's ín the gárden, Jéan.
JEAN: Whát is she dóing?
JACK: She's sítting under the trée.
JEAN: Is Tím in the gárden, tóo?
JACK: Yés, he ís.
He's clímbing the trée.
JEAN: I bég your párdon?
Whó is clímbing the trée?
JACK: Tím is.
JEAN: Whát abóut the dóg?
JACK: The dóg's in the gárden, tóo.
It's rúnning acróss the gráss.
It's rúnning áfter a cát.

Lesson 32　What is he/she/it doing?

20,000

Miss Grey is typing
a letter.

30,000

She is emptying
a basket.

40,000

Mr Richards is opening
the window.

50,000

My mother is making
the bed.

60,000

Sally is shutting
the door.

70,000

It is eating
a bone.

80,000

My sister is looking
at a picture.

90,000

Jack is reading
a magazine.

100,000

He is cleaning
his teeth.

200,000

She is dusting
the dressing-table.

300,000

Mrs Ford is cooking
a meal.

400,000

The cat is drinking
its milk.

500,000

Bessie is sweeping the floor.

600,000

Tim is sharpening a pencil.

700,000

He is turning on the light.

800,000

The girl is turning
off the tap.

900,000

The boy is putting
on his shirt.

1,000,000

Mrs Jones is taking
off her coat.

Exercise　*Look at this:*
Do these in the same way:

Sweep the floor! She *is sweeping it.*

Open the window! He . . .
Sharpen this pencil! She . .
Dust the sideboard! She . . .

Empty the basket! She . . .
Look at the picture! He . . .

It is a fíne dáy todáy.
There are some clóuds in the ský,
but the sún is shíning.
Mŕ Jónes is wíth his fámily.
They are wálking óver the brídge.
There are some bóats on the ríver.
Mŕ Jónes and his wífe are lóoking at them.
Sálly is lóoking at a bíg shíp.
The shíp is góing únder the brídge.
Tím is lóoking at an áeroplane.
The áeroplane is flýing óver the ríver.

Lesson **34** What are they doing?

220,231

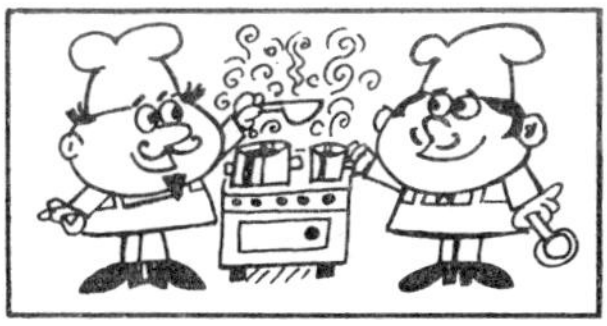

cooking

331,342

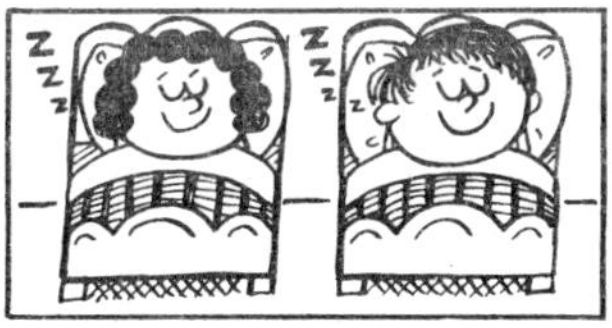

sleeping

442,453

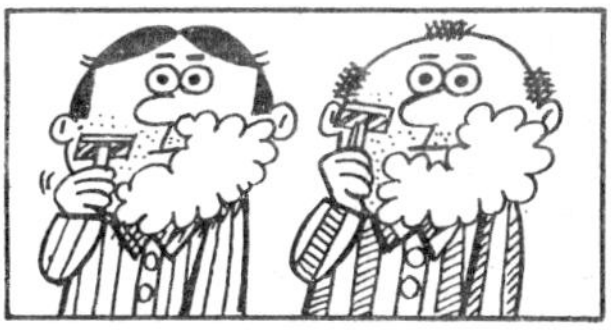

shaving

553,564

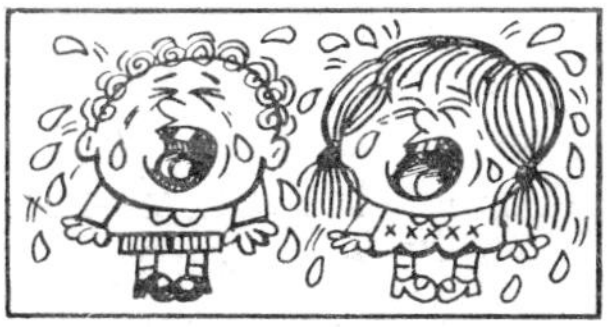

crying

664,675

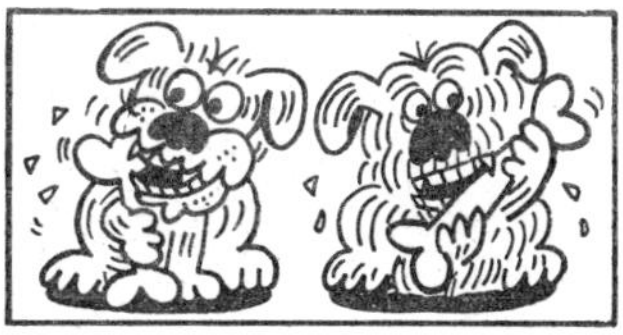

eating

775,786

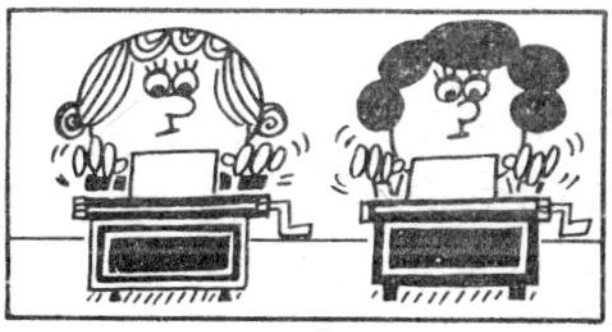

typing

886,897

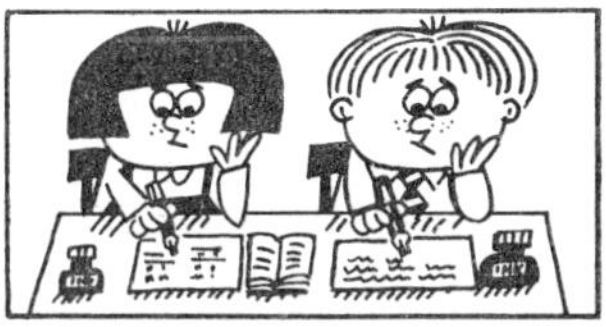

doing

997,998

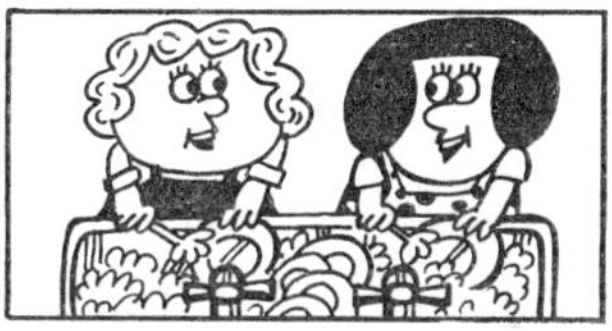

washing

1,000,001

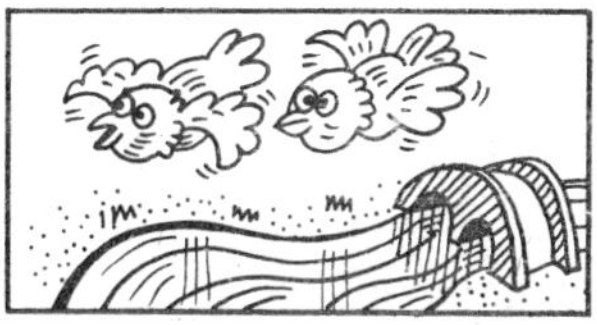

flying

1,100,000

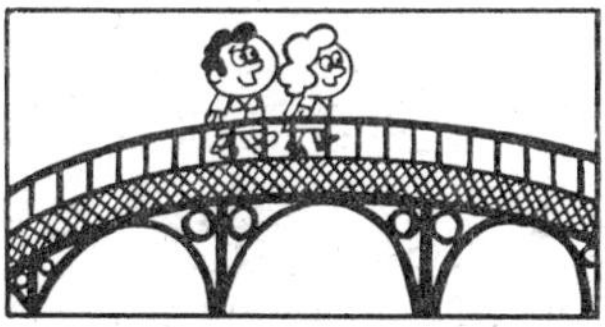

walking

1,500,000

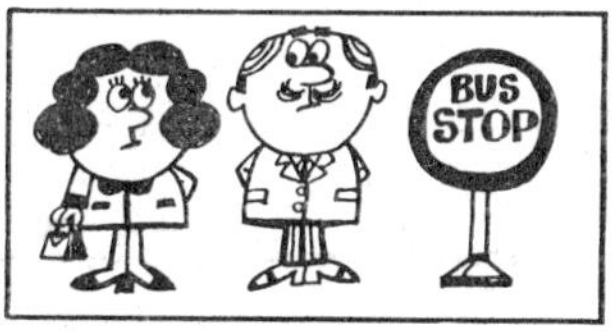

waiting

2,000,000

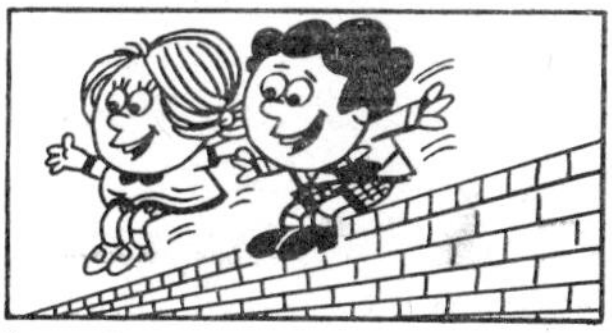

jumping

Exercise

Look at this:

take – tak~~e~~ing
Take . . . He is taking his book.

Do these in the same way:

Type . . .	She is . . . a letter.
Make . . .	She is . . . the bed.
Come . . .	He is . . .
Shine . . .	The sun is . . .
Give . . .	He is . . . me some magazines.

Lesson 35

This is a phótograph of our víllage.
Óur víllage is in a válley.
It is betwéen twó hílls.
The víllage is on a ríver.

Hére is anóther phótograph of the víllage.
My wífe and Í are wálking
alóng the bánks of the ríver.
We are on the léft.
There is a bóy in the wáter.
He is swímming acróss the ríver.

Hére is anóther phótograph.
Thís is the schóol búilding.
It is besíde a párk.
The párk is on the ríght.
Some chíldren are cóming óut of the búilding.
Sóme of them are góing ínto the párk.

Lesson **36**   Where . . . ?

1 one	2 two	3 three
going into	going out of	sitting beside
4 four	5 five	6 six
walking across	running along	jumping off
7 seven	8 eight	9 nine
walking between	sitting near	flying under
10 ten	11 eleven	12 twelve
flying over	sitting on	reading in

Exercise

Look at this:

> put – putting
> Put . . .   He is *putting* on his coat.

Do these in the same way:

Swim . . .   He is . . . across the river.
Sit . . .   She is . . . on the grass.
Run . . .   The cat is . . . along the wall.

Lesson **37**

FRED: Yóu're wórking hárd, Géorge.
       Whát are you dóing?
GEORGE: I'm máking a bóokcáse.

GEORGE: Gíve me thát hámmer pléase, Fréd.
FRED: Whích hámmer?
       Thís óne?

GEORGE: Nó, nót thát óne.
       The bíg óne.

FRED: Hére you áre.
GEORGE: Thánks, Fréd.

FRED: Whát are you góing to dó nów, Géorge?
GEORGE: I'm góing to páint it.

FRED: Whát cólour
       are you góing to páint it?
GEORGE: I'm góing to páint it pínk.
FRED: Pínk!

GEORGE: Thís bóokcáse ísn't for mé.
       It's for my dáughter, Súsan.
       Pínk's her fávourite cólour.

Lesson 38　What are you going to do?
What are you doing now?

one

I am going to shave.

two

Now I am shaving.

three

I'm going to wait for a bus.

four

Now I'm waiting for a bus.

five

We are going to do our homework.

six

Now we are doing our homework.

seven

I'm going to paint this bookcase.

eight

Now I'm painting this bookcase.

nine

We're going to listen to the radio.

ten

Now we're listening to the radio.

eleven

I'm going to wash the dishes.

twelve

Now I'm washing the dishes.

Exercise
Look at this:

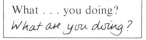

| What . . . you doing? |
| *What are you doing?* |

| We . . . reading. |
| *We are reading.* |

Copy this. Put in am, is *or* are.
What . . . you doing?　We . . . reading.
What . . . they doing?　They . . . doing their homework.
What . . . he doing?　He . . . working hard.
What . . . you doing?　I . . . washing the dishes.

Lesson 39

JOHN: Whát are you góing to dó
with that váse, Máry?

MARY: I'm góing to pút it
on the rádio, Jóhn.

JOHN: Dón't do thát.
Gíve it to mé.

MARY: Whát are you góing to dó with it?
JOHN: I'm góing to pút it hére,
in frónt of the wíndow.

MARY: Bé cáreful!
Dón't dróp it!

MARY: Dón't put it thére, Jóhn.
Pút it hére,
on thís shélf.

JOHN: Thére we áre!
It's a lóvely váse.
MARY: Thóse flówers are lóvely, tóo.

Lesson **40**   **What are you going to do?**
I'm going to . . .

13 thirteen	14 fourteen	15 fifteen	16 sixteen

put it . . . !	take it . . . !	turn it . . . !	turn it . . . !

What are you going to do with that/those . . .
I'm going to give/show/send/take . . .

17 seventeen	18 eighteen	19 nineteen	20 twenty

to my daughter	to my grandmother	to my father	to my mother

30 thirty	40 forty	50 fifty	60 sixty

to the children	to my wife	to my grandfather	to my sister

Exercise
Look at this:

Give me that vase. *Give that vase to me.*

Change these in the same way:
Send George that letter.
Take her those flowers.
Show me that picture.
Give Mrs Jones these books.
Give the children these ice-creams.

Lesson **41**

JOHN: Ís that bag héavy, Máry?
MARY: Nót véry.
JOHN: Hére!
       Pút it on thís cháir.
       What's ín it?

MARY: A píece of chéese.

A lóaf of bréad.

A bár of sóap.

A bár of chócolate.

A bóttle of mílk.

A póund of súgar.

Hálf a póund of cóffee.

A quárter of a póund of téa.

And a tín of tobácco.
JOHN: Ís that tín of tobácco for mé?
MARY: Wéll, it's cértainly nót for mé!

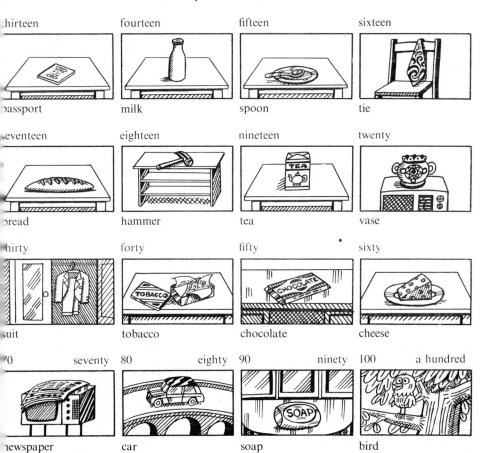

thirteen   fourteen   fifteen   sixteen

passport   milk   spoon   tie

seventeen   eighteen   nineteen   twenty

bread   hammer   tea   vase

thirty   forty   fifty   sixty

suit   tobacco   chocolate   cheese

70   seventy   80   eighty   90   ninety   100   a hundred

newspaper   car   soap   bird

Exercise

Look at these:

> There's *a* photograph on the desk.
> Is there *any* milk in the bottle?
> There isn't *any* milk in the bottle.
> There's *some* milk in that cup.

Copy this. Put in a, any *or* some.
Is there . . . bread in the kitchen?
There's . . . loaf on the table.
There's . . . coffee on the table, too.
There isn't . . . chocolate on the table.
There's . . . spoon on that dish.
Is there . . . soap on the dressing-table?

Lesson 43

MARY: Cán you máke the téa, Jóhn?
JOHN: Yés, of cóurse I cán, Máry.

JOHN: Ís there ány wáter in thís kéttle?
MARY: Yés, there ís.

JOHN: Whére's the téa, déar?
MARY: It's óver thére,
behínd the téapot.

MARY: Cán you sée it?
JOHN: I can sée the téapot,
but I cán't see the téa.

MARY: Thére it ís!
It's in frónt of you!
JOHN: Áh yés, I can sée it nów.

JOHN: Whére are the téacups?
MARY: There are sóme in the cúpboard.

MARY: Cán you fínd them?
JOHN: Yés. Hére they áre.

MARY: Húrry up, Jóhn!
The kéttle's bóiling!

Are there any . . . ?
Is there any . . . ?

seventy

bread on the table

eighty

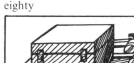

hammers behind that box

ninety

milk in front of the door

hundred

soap on the sideboard

two hundred

newspapers behind that vase

three hundred

water in those glasses

four hundred

tea in those tea cups

five hundred

teacups in front of that kettle

six hundred

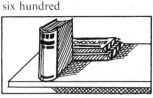

chocolate behind that book

seven hundred

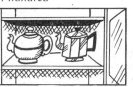

teapots in the cupboard

eight hundred

cars in front of that building

nine hundred

coffee on the table.

Exercise

Look at these:

glass – glasses; book – books; housewife – housewives.

Now look at this:

I can see some cups, but I can't see any . . . (glass).
I can see some cups, but I can't see any glasses.

Do these in the same way:
I can see some spoons, but I can't see any . . . (knife).
I can see some hammers, but I can't see any . . . (box).
I can see some coffee, but I can't see any . . . (loaf) of bread.
I can see some cupboards, but I can't see any . . . (shelf).
I can see Mr Jones and Mr Brown, but I can't see their . . . (wife)
I can see some cups, but I can't see any . . . (dish).
I can see some cars, but I can't see any . . . (bus).

Lesson **45**

THE BOSS:	Cán you cóme hére a mínute pléase, Bób?	
BOB:	Yés, sír?	

THE BOSS:	Whére's Míss Jónes?	
BOB:	She's néxt dóor. She's ín her óffice, sír.	

THE BOSS:	Cán she týpe thís létter for me? Ásk her pléase.	
BOB:	Yés, sír.	

BOB:	Cán you týpe thís létter for the bóss pléase, Miss Jónes?	
MISS JONES:	Yés, of cóurse I cán.	

BOB:	Hére you áre.	
MISS JONES:	Thánk you, Bób.	

MISS JONES:	Bób!	
BOB:	Yés? Whát's the mátter?	
MISS JONES:	I cán't týpe thís létter.	

MISS JONES:	I cán't réad it! The bóss's hándwriting is térrible!	

1000
thousand

I can put my hat on,
but I can't put my coat on.

10,000
ten thousand

I can paint this bookcase,
but I can't paint this room.

210,000
two hundred and ten thousand

I can read this book,
but I can't read that magazine.

500,000
five hundred thousand

I can make cakes,
but I can't make biscuits.

5000
five thousand

I can see that aeroplane,
but I can't see a bird.

100,000
a hundred thousand

I can lift that chair,
but I can't lift this table.

350,000
three hundred and fifty thousand

I can jump off this box,
but I can't jump off that wall.

1,000,000
a million

I can put the vase on this table,
but I can't put it on that shelf.

Exercise
Look at these:

| He is taking his book. | *He can take his book.* |
| She is putting on her coat. | *She can put on her coat.* |

Change these in the same way:

They are typing these letters.
She is making the bed.
You are swimming across the river.
We are coming now.
We are running across the park.
He is sitting on the grass.
I am giving him some chocolate.

MRS YOUNG: Dó you líke cóffee, Mŕs Príce?
MRS PRICE: Yés, I dó.

MRS YOUNG: Dó·you wánt a cúp?
MRS PRICE: Yés, pléase, Mŕs Yóung.

MRS YOUNG: Dó you wánt any súgar?
MRS PRICE: Yés, pléase.

MRS YOUNG: Dó you wánt any mílk?
MRS PRICE: Nó, thánk you.
Í dón't líke mílk in my cóffee.
Í like bláck cóffee.

MRS YOUNG: Dó you líke bíscuits?
MRS PRICE: Yés, I dó.

MRS YOUNG: Dó you wánt one?
MRS PRICE: Yés, pléase.

Do you like . . . ?
Do you want . . . ?

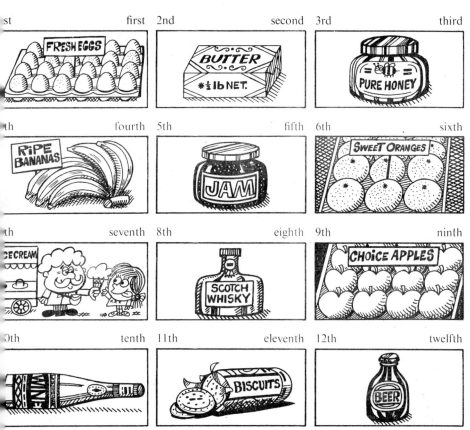

st   first   2nd   second   3rd   third

th   fourth   5th   fifth   6th   sixth

th   seventh   8th   eighth   9th   ninth

)th   tenth   11th   eleventh   12th   twelfth

xercise

opy these. Put in off, over, between, along, in front of, behind, under, *or* across.

he aeroplane is flying . . . the village.
he ship is going . . . the bridge.
he children are swimming . . . the river.
wo cats are running . . . the wall.
he boy is jumping . . . the tree.
he girl is sitting . . . her mother and her father.
he teacher is standing . . . the blackboard.
he blackboard is . . . the teacher.

Lesson **49**

BUTCHER: Dó you wánt any méat todáy,
Mrs Bírd?
MRS BIRD: Yés, pléase.

BUTCHER: Dó you wánt béef or lámb?
MRS BIRD: Béef, pléase.

BUTCHER: Thís lámb's véry góod.
MRS BIRD: Í like lámb,
but my húsband dóesn't.

BUTCHER: Whát abóut some stéak?
Thís is a níce píece.
MRS BIRD: Gíve me thát piece pléase.

MRS BIRD: And a póund of mínce, tóo.

BUTCHER: Dó you wánt a chícken, Mrs Bírd?
They're véry níce.
MRS BIRD: Nó, thánk you.

MRS BIRD: My húsband líkes stéak,
but he dóesn't líke chícken.
BUTCHER: To téll you the trúth, Mrs Bírd,
Í don't like chicken, éither!

Lesson **50** He likes . . .
but he doesn't like . . .

13th   thirteenth

14th   fourteenth

15th   fifteenth

16th   sixteenth

17th   seventeenth

18th   eighteenth

19th   nineteenth

20th   twentieth

21st   twenty-first

22nd   twenty-second

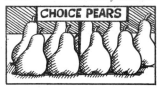

23rd   twenty-third

24th   twenty-fourth

Exercise

Look at this: | She likes potatoes, but I . . . *She likes potatoes, but I don't.*

Copy these. Put in am not, aren't, isn't, can't, don't, *or* doesn't.
He likes coffee, but I . . .
She likes tea, but he . . .
He is eating some bread, but she . . .
She can type very well, but he . . .
They are working hard, but we . . .
He is reading a magazine, but I . . .

Lesson 51

HANS: Whére do you cóme fróm?
DIMITRI: I cóme from Gréece.
HANS: Whát's the clímate líke
in yóur cóuntry?
DIMITRI: It's véry pléasant.

HANS: Whát's the wéather líke in spríng?
DIMITRI: It's óften wíndy in Márch.
It's álways wárm in Ápril and Máy,
but it ráins sometimes.

HANS: Whát's it líke in súmmer?
DIMITRI: It's álways hót
in Júne, Julý and Áugust.
The sún shínes évery dáy.

HANS: Is it cóld or wárm in áutumn?
DIMITRI: It's álways wárm
in Septémber and Octóber.
It's óften cóld in Novémber
and it ráins sometimes.

HANS: Is it véry cóld in wínter?
DIMITRI: It's óften cóld
in Decémber, Jánuary and Fébruary.
It snóws sometimes.

Lesson 52 What nationality are they?
Where do they come from?

20th

I'm American.
I come from America.

21st

He's Brazilian.
He comes from Brazil.

22nd

She's Dutch.
She comes from Holland.

23rd

We're English.
We come from England.

24th

They're French.
They come from France.

25th

You're German.
You come from Germany.

26th

He's Greek.
He comes from Greece.

27th

You're Italian.
You come from Italy.

28th

We're Norwegian.
We come from Norway.

29th

They're Russian.
They come from Russia.

30th

She's Spanish.
She comes from Spain.

31st

I'm Swedish.
I come from Sweden.

Exercise

Look at this:

> I come from England, but Stella . . . from Spain.
> *I come from England, but Stella comes from Spain.*

Do these in the same way:
We come from Germany, but Dimitri . . . from Greece.
I like cold weather, but he . . . warm weather.
He comes from America, but she . . . from England.
She doesn't like the winter, but she . . . the summer.
I come from Norway, but you . . . from Sweden.
Stella comes from Spain, but Hans and Carl . . . from Germany.
We don't come from Spain. We . . . from Brazil.

Lesson **53**

HANS: Whére do you cóme fróm?
JIM: I cóme from Éngland.
HANS: Whát's the clímate líke
in yóur cóuntry?
JIM: It's míld,
but it's nót álways pléasant.

JIM: The wéather's óften cóld in the Nórth
and wíndy in the Éast.
It's óften wét in the Wést
and sómetimes wárm in the Sóuth.

HANS: Whích séasons do you líke bést?
JIM: I like spríng and súmmer.
The dáys are lóng
and the níghts are shórt.
The sún ríses éarly
and séts láte.

JIM: I dón't líke áutumn and wínter.
The dáys are shórt
and the níghts are lóng.
The sún ríses láte
and séts éarly.
Óur clímate is nót véry góod,
but it's cértainly ínteresting.
It's our fávourite súbject
of conversátion.

Lesson 54 What nationality are they?
Where do they come from?

20th

I'm Australian.
I come from Australia.

30th

He's Austrian.
He comes from Austria.

40th

He's Canadian.
He comes from Canada.

50th

We're Chinese.
We come from China.

60th

They're Danish.
They come from Denmark.

70th

You're Finnish.
You come from Finland.

80th

She's Indian.
She comes from India.

90th

You're Japanese.
You come from Japan.

100th

We're Nigerian.
We come from Nigeria.

101st

They're Polish.
They come from Poland.

102nd

She's Turkish.
She comes from Turkey.

103rd

I'm Yugoslavian.
I come from Yugoslavia.

Exercise

Look at this:

The sun rises early.	*Does the sun rise early?*
	The sun doesn't rise early.

Do these in the same way:

The sun sets late.   . . .

                            . . .

He likes ice-cream.   . . .

                            . . .

Mrs Jones wants a biscuit. . . .

                            . . .

Jim comes from England.   . . .

                            . . .

Lesson 55

The Sáwyers líve at 87 Kíng Stréet.

In the mórning, Mr Sáwyer góes to wórk
and the chíldren go to schóol.
Their fáther tákes them to schóol évery dáy.

Mŕs Sáwyer stáys at hóme évery dáy.
She dóes the hóusework.

She álways éats her lúnch at nóon.

In the afternóon,
she úsually sées her fríends.
They óften drínk téa togéther.

In the évening,
the chíldren cóme hóme from schóol.
They arríve hóme éarly.

Mŕ Sáwyer cómes hóme from wórk.
He arríves hóme láte.

At níght,
the chíldren álways dó their hómework.
Thén they gó to béd.
Mŕ Sáwyer úsually réads his néwspaper,
but sómetimes hé and his wífe wátch télevisìon.

Lesson 56   What do they usually do?

every day   in the morning   at noon
               in the afternoon   at night
               in the evening

1st

dusts

2nd

makes

3rd

shaves

4th

listen

21st

cleans

22nd

go

23rd

washes

24th

type

31st

drinks

32nd

watch

33rd

eats

34th

reads

Exercise
Look at this:

> She wash . . . the dishes every day.
> *She washes the dishes every day*

Copy this. Add s *or* es *where necessary:*
The children go . . . to school in the morning.
Their father take . . . them to school.
Mrs Sawyer stay . . . at home.
She do . . . the housework.
She always eat . . . her lunch at noon.

It is éight o'clóck.
The chíldren gó to schóol by cár
évery dáy,
but todáy,
they are góing to schóol on fóot.

It is tén o'clóck.
Mŕs Sáwyer úsually stáys at hóme
in the mórning,
but this mórning,
she is góing to the shóps.

It is fóur o'clóck.
Ín the áfternóon,
Mrs Sáwyer úsually drínks téa
in the líving-róom.
But this áfternóon,
she is drínking téa in the gárden.

It is síx o'clóck.
Ín the évening,
the chíldren úsually dó their hómework,
but this évening,
they are nót dóing their hómework.
At the móment,
they are pláying in the gárden.

It is níne o'clóck.
Mr Sáwyer úsually réads his néwspaper
at níght.
But he's nót réading his néwspaper toníght.
At the móment,
he's réading an ínteresting bóok.

Lesson 58   What's the time?

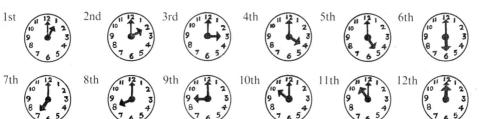

1st   2nd   3rd   4th   5th   6th

7th   8th   9th   10th   11th   12th

They usually . . . but today, they are . . .

13th

He usually shaves at
7.0 o'clock every day,

14th

but today, he . . .

15th

She usually drinks tea in the morning,

16th

but this morning, she . . .

17th

They usually play in the
garden in the afternoon,

18th

but this afternoon, they . . .

19th

I usually cook a meal in the evening,

20th

but this evening, I . . .

21st

We usually watch television at night,

22nd

but tonight, we . . .

Exercise
Look at this:

| He usually shaves at 7.0. | *He usually shaves at 7.0,* |
| but today, he . . . at 8.0. | *but today, he is shaving at 8.0.* |

Do these in the same way:

She usually drinks tea in the morning, but this morning, she . . . coffee.
They usually play in the garden in the afternoon, but this afternoon, they . . . in the park.
She usually washes the dishes at night, but tonight she . . . clothes.

Lesson **59**

LADY: I wánt some énvelopes pléase.
STATIONER: Dó you wánt
the lárge síze, or the smáll síze?
LADY: The lárge síze pléase.

LADY: Háve you any wríting-páper?
STATIONER: Yés, we háve.

STATIONER: I háven't any smáll páds.
I ónly háve lárge ones.
Dó you wánt a pád?
LADY: Yés, pléase.

LADY: And I wánt some
bláck ínk and some glúe.
STATIONER: A bóttle of ínk
and a bóttle of glúe.

LADY: And I wánt
a lárge bóx of chálk, tóo.
STATIONER: I ónly háve smáll boxes.
Dó you wánt one?
LADY: Nó, thánk you.

STATIONER: Is thát áll?
LADY: Thát's áll, thánk you.

STATIONER: Whát élse do you wánt?
LADY: I wánt my chánge.

Lesson 60　What's the time?

1st　2nd　3rd　4th　5th　6th

7th　8th　9th　10th　11th　12th

Have you any . . . ?

13th	14th	15th	16th	17th	18th
cheese	butter	eggs	jam	honey	bread

19th	20th	21st	22nd	23rd	24th
biscuits	potatoes	tomatoes	peas	beans	cabbages

25th	26th	27th	28th	29th	30th
lettuces	bananas	grapes	peaches	steak	mince

31st	32nd	33rd	34th	35th	36th
chicken	whisky	beer	wine	tobacco	soap

Exercise

Look at these:

> I haven't any *banana*, but I have some *peach*.
> *I haven't any bananas, but I have some peaches.*
> I haven't any *coffee*, but I have some *milk*.
> *I haven't any coffee, but I have some milk.*

Copy these. Add s *or* es *where necessary.*
I haven't any *grape*, but I have some *peach*.
I haven't any *tomato*, but I have some *potato*.
I haven't any *mince*, but I have some *steak*.
I haven't any *glue*, but I have some *ink*.
I haven't any *envelope*, but I have some *writing-paper*.

Lesson 61

MR WILLIAMS: Whére's Jímmy?
MRS WILLIAMS: Hé's in béd.
MR WILLIAMS: Whát's the mátter with him?
MRS WILLIAMS: He féels íll.

MR WILLIAMS: He lóoks íll.
MRS WILLIAMS: We must cáll the dóctor.
MR WILLIAMS: Yés, we múst.

MR WILLIAMS: Cán you remémber
the dóctor's télephone númber?
MRS WILLIAMS: Yés.
Ít's 09754.

DOCTOR: Ópen your móuth, Jímmy.
Shów me your tóngue.
Sáy, 'Áh'.

MR WILLIAMS: Whát's the mátter with him,
dóctor?
DOCTOR: He has a bád cóld,
Mr Wílliams,
so he must stáy in béd
for a wéek.

MRS WILLIAMS: That's góod néws for Jímmy.
DOCTOR: Góod néws?
Whý?
MR WILLIAMS: Becáuse he dóesn't líke schóol!

Lesson **62**   What's the matter with them?
What must they do?

41st

She has a headache.
So she must take an aspirin.

52nd

George has an ear-ache.
So he must see a doctor.

63rd

He has toothache.
So he must see a dentist.

74th

Jane has a stomach-ache.
So she must drink some medicine.

85th

Tom has a temperature.
So he must go to bed.

96th

Frank has flu.
So he must stay in bed.

107th

Jimmy has measles.
So we must call the doctor.

118th

Susan has mumps.
So we must call the doctor.

Exercise

Look at these:

| I have a headache. | He has a headache. |
| I must stay at home. | He must stay at home. |

Write these again. Begin each sentence with He.

I have a cold.   He ...
I can't go to work.   ...
I am not well.   ...
I feel ill.   ...
I must see a doctor.   ...
I do not like doctors. ...

Lesson **63**

DOCTOR:	Hów's Jímmy todáy?	1
MRS WILLIAMS:	He's bétter thánk you, dóctor.	
DOCTOR:	Cán I sée him pléase, Mrs Wílliams?	
MRS WILLIAMS:	Cértainly, dóctor. Cóme upstáirs.	

DOCTOR: You look véry wéll, Jímmy.
You are bétter nów,
but you mústn't get up yét.
You must stáy in béd
for anóther twó dáys.

2

DOCTOR: The bóy mústn't
gó to school yét, Mrs Wílliams.
And he mústn't éat rích fóod.

MRS WILLIAMS: Hás he a témperature, dóctor?

DOCTOR: Nó, he hásn't.

MRS WILLIAMS: Múst he stáy in béd?

DOCTOR: Yés.
He must remáin in béd
for anóther two dáys.
He can gét úp
for about twó hóurs éach dáy,
but you múst kéep the
róom wárm.

3

DOCTOR: Whére's Mr Wílliams this
évening?

MRS WILLIAMS: He's in béd, dóctor.
Cán you sée him pléase?
Hé has a bád cóld, tóo!

4

Lesson **64** Don't . . . !
You mustn't . . . !

110

. . . take any
aspirins!

221

. . . drink this
medicine!

332

. . . call the
doctor!

443

. . . play with
matches!

554

. . . talk in the
library!

665

. . . make a noise!

776

. . . drive so
quickly!

887

. . . lean out of
the window!

998

. . . break that vase!

Exercise
Look at this:

> I mustn't take any aspirins.
> *Jimmy mustn't take any aspirins.*

Write these again. Begin each sentence with Jimmy.
I am better now but I mustn't get up yet.
I have a cold and I must stay in bed.
I can get up for two hours each day.
I often read in bed.
I listen to the radio, too.
I don't feel ill now.

Lesson **65**

FATHER: Whát are you góing to dó
this évening, Bétty?
BETTY: I'm góing to méet some fríends, Dád.

FATHER: You mústn't cóme hóme láte.
You must bé hóme at hálf pást tén.
BETTY: I cán't get hóme só éarly, Dád!

BETTY: Cán I háve the kéy
to the frónt dóor, pléase?
FATHER: Nó, you cán't.

MOTHER: Bétty's éighteen yéars óld, Tóm.
She's nót a báby.
Gíve her the kéy.
She álways comes home éarly.
FATHER: Oh, áll ríght!

FATHER: Hére you áre.
But you mústn't cóme hóme
after a quárter pást eléven.
Dó you héar?
BETTY: Yés, Dád.

BETTY: Thánks, Múm.
MOTHER: Thát's all ríght, déar.
Góodbye.
Enjóy yourself!
BETTY: We álways enjóy ourselves, Múm.
Býe, býe.

2nd 3rd 4th 5th 6th

 8th 9th 10th 11th 12th

When's your birthday?
How old are you?

	JULY				
S		7	14	21	28
M	1	8	15	22	29
Tu	2	9	16	23	30
W	3	10	17	24	31
Th	4	11	18	25	
F	5	12	19	26	
S	6	13	20	27	

Enjoy yourself!

13th

Enjoy yourself!
I always enjoy myself.

14th

We're enjoying ourselves.
They're enjoying themselves.

15th

He's enjoying himself.

16th

She's enjoying herself.

Exercise

Copy these. Put in in, at *or* from.
I am going to see him . . . ten o'clock.
It often rains . . . November.
Where do you come . . . ? I come . . . France.
I always go to work . . . the morning.
What's the climate like . . . your country?
It's cold . . . winter and hot . . . summer.

MRS JOHNSON: Húllo, Mrs Wílliams.
Wére you at the bútcher's?
MRS WILLIAMS: Yés, I wás.
Wére yóu at the bútcher's, tóo?
MRS JOHNSON: Nó, I wásn't.
Í was at the gréengrocer's.
Hów's Jímmy todáy?
MRS WILLIAMS: He's véry wéll, thánk you.
MRS JOHNSON: Wás he ábsent from schóol lást wéek?
MRS WILLIAMS: Yés, he wás.
He was ábsent on Mónday, Túesday,
Wédnesday and Thúrsday.
Hów are yóu áll kéeping?
MRS JOHNSON: Véry wéll, thánk you.
We're góing to spénd thrée dáys
in the cóuntry.
We're góing to stáy at my móther's
for the wéek-énd.
MRS WILLIAMS: Fríday, Sáturday and Súnday
in the cóuntry!
Áren't you lúcky!

Lesson **68** What's the time?

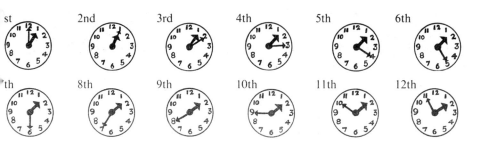

1st 2nd 3rd 4th 5th 6th

7th 8th 9th 10th 11th 12th

Where were you on . . . ?
When were you at . . . ?

Sunday, January 1st

church

Monday, February 2nd

school

Tuesday, March 3rd

the office

Wednesday, April 4th

the butcher's

Thursday, May 5th

the barber's

Friday, June 6th

the baker's

Saturday, July 7th

the dairy

Sunday, August 8th

home

Monday, September 9th

the grocer's

Tuesday, October 10th

the greengrocer's

Wednesday, November 11th

the tobacconist's

Thursday, December 12th

the stationer's

Exercise

Copy these. Put in the where *necessary.*

I was at . . . church on Sunday.
I was at . . . office on Monday.
My son was at . . . school on Tuesday.
My wife was at . . . butcher's on Wednesday.
She was at . . . grocer's on Thursday.
My daughter was in . . . country on Friday.
I was at . . . home on Saturday.

68

Lesson **69**

There is a cár ráce
near óur tówn évery yéar.
In Í968,
there was a véry bíg ráce.

There were húndreds of péople thére.
My wífe and Í were at the ráce.
Our fríends, Júlie and Jáck
were thére, tóo.
You can sée us in the crówd.
We are stánding on the léft.

There were twénty cárs in the ráce.
There were Énglish cárs, Frénch cárs,
Gérman cárs, Itálian cárs,
Américan cárs and Japanése cárs.

It was an excíting fínish.
The wínner was Bílly Stéwart.
He was in cár númber fíftéen.
Fíve óther cárs were just behínd him.

On the way hóme,
my wífe sáid to me,
"Dón't dríve so quíckly!
You're nót Bílly Stéwart!"

ON

Monday	Tuesday	Wednesday	Thursday	Friday	Saturday
STATIONER	GREENGROCER	BARBER	BUTCHER	GROCER	DAIRY

at:

ON

Jan. 21st	Feb. 22nd	March 23rd	April 24th	May 25th	June 26th
	SCHOOL	OFFICE / OUT	BAKER	HOME SWEET HOME	TOBACCONIST

at:

IN

July	August	September	October	November	December
AUSTRALIA	AUSTRIA	CANADA	CHINA	DENMARK	FINLAND

in:

IN

1931	1947	1952	1956	1960	1967
INDIA	JAPAN	NIGERIA	POLAND	TURKEY	YUGOSLAVIA

in:

Exercise

Copy these. Put in at, on *or* in.
We were . . . the stationer's . . . Monday.
We were there . . . four o'clock.
They were . . . Australia . . . September.
They were there . . . spring.
. . November 25th, they were . . . Canada.
They were there . . . 1967.

JANE: Whát's Rón Márston like, Páuline?
PAULINE: He's áwful!
He télephoned me
fóur tímes yésterday,
and thrée tímes
the dáy befóre yésterday.

PAULINE: He télephoned the óffice
yésterday mórning
and yésterday afternóon.
My bóss ánswered the télephone.

JANE: Whát did your bóss sáy to him?
PAULINE: He sáid, "Míss Whíte is týping létters.
She cán't spéak to you nów!"

PAULINE: Thén I arríved home
at síx o'clóck yésterday évening.
He télephoned agáin.
But I dídn't ánswer the phóne!

JANE: Díd he télephone agáin lást níght?
PAULINE: Yés, he díd.
He télephoned at níne o'clóck.

JANE: Whát did you sáy to him?
PAULINE: I sáid, "Thís is Páuline's móther.
Pléase dón't télephone
my dáughter agáin!"

JANE: Díd he télephone agáin?
PAULINE: Nó, he dídn't!

TODAY	YESTERDAY	THE DAY BEFORE YESTERDAY
this morning	yesterday morning	the day before yesterday in the morning
this afternoon	yesterday afternoon	the day before yesterday in the afternoon
this evening	yesterday evening	the day before yesterday in the evening
tonight	last night	the night before last

When did you . . . ?

1st	2nd	3rd	4th	5th

aired	cleaned	opened	sharpened	turned on

6th	7th	8th	9th	10th

listened	boiled	arrived	played	stayed

11th	12th	13th	14th	15th

shaved	climbed	telephoned	called	emptied

Exercise
Look at this:

She is airing the room now. She . . . it yesterday.

> *She aired it yesterday*

Do these in the same way:
It is raining now.   It . . . yesterday.
It is snowing now.   It . . . yesterday.
She is boiling some eggs.   She . . . some yesterday.
We are enjoying our lunch.   We . . . it yesterday, too.
They are hurrying to work.   They . . . to work yesterday, too.

Can you do this Test?

I. Dictation.

II. Look at this:

> I am tired.　　　　　　*He is tired.*

Write these again. Begin each sentence with *He*.

1. I must call the doctor.　　*He ...*
2. I am going to telephone him.　...
3. I can go with her.　　　　...
4. I have a new car.　　　　...
5. I come from America.　　...
6. I am American.　　　　...
7. I like ice-cream.　　　...
8. I want a newspaper.　　...
9. I was at school yesterday.　...
10. I don't live here.　　　...

III. Look at this:

> *There is a pencil* on the desk.
> *There are some pencils on the desk.*

Write these again. Begin each sentence with *There are* . . .

1. *There is a watch* on the table.
2. *There is a knife* near that tin.
3. *There is a policeman* in the kitchen.
4. *There is a cup* on the table.
5. *There is a letter* on the shelf.
6. *There is a peach* on the desk.
7. *There is a passport* on the shelf
8. *There is a dish* in the cupboard
9. *There is a tree* in the garden.
10. *There is a boat* on the river.

IV. Put in *a, some* or *any:*

1. I have . . . new car.
2. There are . . . clouds in the sky.
3. There is . . . milk in the bottle.
4. Is there . . . chocolate on the shelf?
5. There is . . . bar of chocolate on the table.
6. I want . . . loaf of bread, please
7. Do you want . . . bread?
8. No, I don't want . . . bread.
9. I want . . . tea.
10. I want . . . biscuits, too.

V. Put in *in, at, from* or *on:*

1. He is going to telephone . . . five o'clock.
2. My birthday is . . . May 21st.
3. It is always cold . . . February.
4. She isn't French. She comes . . . Spain.
5. My father was there . . . 1942.
6. Were you . . . school yesterday?
7. He doesn't live here. He lives . . . England.
8. They always do their homework . . . the evening.
9. Can you come . . . Monday?
10. She's not here. She's . . . the butcher's.

VI. Put in *across, over, between, off, along, in, on, into, out of,* or *under.*
  1. The aeroplane is flying . . . the village.
  2. The ship is going . . . the bridge.
  3. The boy is swimming . . . the river.
  4. Two cats are running . . . the wall.
  5. My books are . . . the shelf.
  6. The bottle of milk is . . . the refrigerator.
  7. The boy is jumping . . . the tree.
  8. Mary is sitting . . . her mother and her father.
  9. It is 9.0 o'clock. The children are going . . . class.
  10. It is 4.0 o'clock. The children are coming . . . class.

VII. Look at this:

Take . . .	He is *taking* his book.

Do these in the same way:
  1. Make . . .   She is . . . the bed.
  2. Swim . . .   They are . . . across the river.
  3. Shine . . .   The sun is . . .
  4. Shave . . .   My father is . . .
  5. Run . . .   They are . . . across the park.
  6. Sit . . .   She is . . . in an armchair.
  7. Type . . .   We are . . . letters.
  8. Put . . .   He is . . . on his coat.
  9. Come . . .   I am . . .
  10. Give . . .   I am . . . it to him.

VIII. Look at this:

	He is sitting in an armchair.
QUESTION:	*Is he sitting in an armchair?*
QUESTION:	*Where is he sitting?*
NEGATIVE:	*He isn't sitting in an armchair.*

Do these in the same way:
1. He can come now.
Q: ...
Q: When ...
N: ...

2. There is a newspaper on the desk.
Q: ...
Q: What ...
N: ...

3. He wants a new car.
Q: ...
Q: What ...
N: ...

4. He is going to come now.
Q: ...
Q: When ...
N: ...

5. They like ice-cream.
Q: ...
Q: What ...
N: ...

6. He comes from Germany.
Q: ...
Q: Where ...
N: ...

7. They must go home now.
Q: ...
Q: When ...
N: ...

8. He feels ill.
Q: ...
Q: How ...
N: ...

9. He has a headache.
Q: ...
Q: What ...
N: ...

10. He cleaned his shoes.
Q: ...
Q: When ...
N: ...

74

Lást wéek Mrs Mílls wént to Lóndon.
She dóes not knów Lóndon véry wéll,
and she lóst her wáy.

Súddenly, she sáw a mán
néar a bús-stóp.
"I can ásk him the wáy,"
she sáid to hersélf.

"Excúse me," she sáid.
"Cán you téll me the wáy
to Kíng Stréet pléase?"

The mán smíled pléasantly.
He díd not únderstánd Énglish!
He spóke Gérman.
He was a tóurist.

Thén he pút his hánd
ínto his pócket,
and tóok óut a phráse-bóok.

He ópened the bóok
and fóund a phráse.
He réad the phráse slówly.
"I am sórry," he sáid.
"I dó not spéak Énglish."

Lesson **74**   What did they do?

101

He shaved hurriedly
this morning and
cut himself badly.

102

He took a cake
and ate it quickly.

103

I gave him a glass of water
and he drank it thirstily.

104

I met her in the street
the day before yesterday
and she greeted me warmly.

105

The bus went slowly
yesterday afternoon
and we arrived home late.

106

They worked very hard
this morning.

107

We enjoyed ourselves
very much last night.

108

He swam very well this afternoon.

Exercise

Look at this:

> quick – quickly; thirsty – thirstily; careful – carefully.

Now look at this:

> She smiled . . . (pleasant)   *She smiled pleasantly.*

Do these in the same way:
He read the phrase . . . (slow)
He worked . . . (lazy)
He cut himself . . . (bad)
He worked . . . (careful)
The door opened . . . (sudden)

Lesson **75**

LADY:	Háve you ány shóes líke thése?
SALESMAN:	Whát síze?
LADY:	Síze fíve.
SALESMAN:	Whát cólour?
LADY:	Bláck.
SALESMAN:	I'm sórry.
	We háven't ány.
LADY:	But my síster bóught thís páir
	lást mónth.
SALESMAN:	Díd she búy them hére?
LADY:	Nó, she bóught them
	in the Ú.Ś.Á.
SALESMAN:	We hád some shóes like thóse
	a mónth agó,
	but we háven't ány nów.
LADY:	Cán you gét a páir for me pléase?
SALESMAN:	I'm afráid that I cán't.
	They were ín fáshion lást yéar
	and the yéar before lást.
	But they're nót in fáshion
	thís yéar.

SALESMAN:	Thése shóes are in fáshion nów.
LADY:	Théy lóok véry uncómfortable.
SALESMAN:	They *áre* very uncómfortable.
	But wómen álways wéar
	uncómfortable shóes!

Lesson 76

this week	last week	the week before last
this month	last month	the month before last
this year	last year	the year before last

a minute		two minutes	
an hour		five hours	
a day	AGO	three days	AGO
a week		two weeks	
a month		four months	
a year		six years	

When did you . . . ?

109 looked
110 jumped
111 walked
112 washed
113 worked

114 asked
115 typed
116 watched
117 talked
118 thanked

119 dusted
120 painted
121 waited
122 wanted
123 greeted

Exercise

Look at this:

She *goes* to town every day. *She went to town yesterday.*

Do these in the same way:
She *meets* her friends every day.
They *drink* some milk every day.
He *swims* in the river every day.
She *takes* him to school every day.
He *cuts* himself every morning.

NURSE: Good mórning, Mr Cróft.
MR CROFT: Good mórning, núrse.
            I wánt to sée the déntist, pléase.
NURSE: Háve you an appóintment?
MR CROFT: Nó, I háven't.
NURSE: Ís it úrgent?
MR CROFT: Yés, it ís.
            It's véry úrgent.
            I féel áwful.
            I háve térrible tóothache.
NURSE: Cán you cóme at Í0 a.m.
            on Mónday, Ápril 24th?
MR CROFT: I múst sée the déntist nów, núrse.
NURSE: The déntist is véry búsy
            at the móment.
            Cán you cóme at 2.0 p.m.?
MR CROFT: That's véry láte.
            Cán't the déntist sée me nów?
NURSE: I'm afráid that he cán't, Mr Cróft.
            Cán't you wáit till this áfternóon?
MR CROFT: Í can wáit, but my tóothache cán't!

Lesson 78 When did you . . . ?

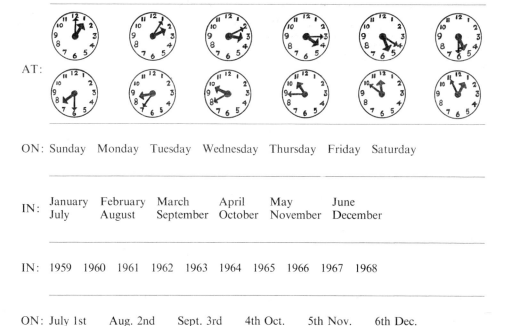

ON: Sunday Monday Tuesday Wednesday Thursday Friday Saturday

IN:
January February March   April   May   June
July   August   September October November December

IN: 1959 1960 1961 1962 1963 1964 1965 1966 1967 1968

ON: July 1st   Aug. 2nd   Sept. 3rd   4th Oct.   5th Nov.   6th Dec.

Exercise

Look at this:

She goes to town every day. She *went* to town yesterday.

Do these in the same way:
He buys a new car every year. He . . . a new car last year.
She airs the room every day. She . . . it this morning.
He often loses his pen. He . . . his pen this morning.
He always listens to the news. He . . . to the news yesterday.
She empties this basket every day. She . . . it yesterday.

Lesson **79**

TOM: Whát are you dóing, Péggy?
PEGGY: I'm máking a shópping-líst, Tóm.

TOM: Whát do we néed?
PEGGY: We néed a lót of thíngs thís wéek.

PEGGY: I múst gó to the grócer's.
We háven't gót much téa or cóffee,
and we háven't gót any súgar or jám.

TOM: Whát about végetables?
PEGGY: I múst gó to the gréengrócer's.
We háven't gót many tomátoes,
but we've gót a lót of potátoes.

PEGGY: I múst gó to the bútcher's, tóo.
We néed some méat.
We háven't gót any méat at áll.

TOM: Háve we gót any béer and wíne?
PEGGY: Nó, we háven't.
And I'm nót góing to gét ány!

TOM: I hópe that you've gót some móney.
PEGGY: I háven't gót múch.
TOM: Well Í háven't gót múch éither!

Lesson **80**   I must go to the . . .

GROCER'S to get some GROCERIES:

120	121	122	123	124	125

cheese   eggs   butter   honey   jam   biscuits

GREENGROCER'S to get some FRUIT and VEGETABLES:

226   227   228   229   230   231

pears   oranges   bananas   beans   peas   cabbages

BUTCHER'S to get some MEAT:

332   333   334   335   336

lamb   beef   steak   mince   chicken

STATIONER'S to get some STATIONERY:

437   438   439   440

ink   glue   envelopes   writing-paper

NEWSAGENT'S to get some: BAKER'S to get some:

541   542   543   544

newspapers   magazines   bread   cakes

TOBACCONIST'S to get   CHEMIST'S to get some:
some:

645   646   647   648

cigarettes   tobacco   aspirins   medicine

Exercise
Look at this:

I haven't any eggs.	*I haven't got many eggs.*
He hasn't any coffee.	*He hasn't got much coffee.*

Do these in the same way:
I haven't any butter.
You haven't any cigarettes.
We haven't any milk.
She hasn't any biscuits.
They haven't any stationery.

JOHN: Húllo, Péggy!
Whére's Tóm?
PEGGY: He's úpstáirs.
He's háving a báth.

PEGGY: Tóm!
TOM: Yés?
PEGGY: Jóhn's hére.
TOM: I'm néarly réady.

TOM: Húllo, Jóhn.
Háve a cígarétte.
JOHN: Nó thanks, Tóm.
TOM: Háve a gláss of whísky then.
JOHN: Ó.Ḱ. Thánks.

TOM: Is dínner réady, Péggy?
PEGGY: It's néarly réady.
We can háve dínner at séven o'clóck.

TOM: Jóhn and Í had lúnch togéther todáy.
We wént to a réstaurant.
PEGGY: Whát did you háve?
TOM: We had róast
béef and potátoes.

PEGGY: Óh!
TOM: Whát's the mátter, Péggy?
PEGGY: Wéll, you're góing to háve
róast béef and potátoes agáin toníght!

Lesson 82   I had . . .

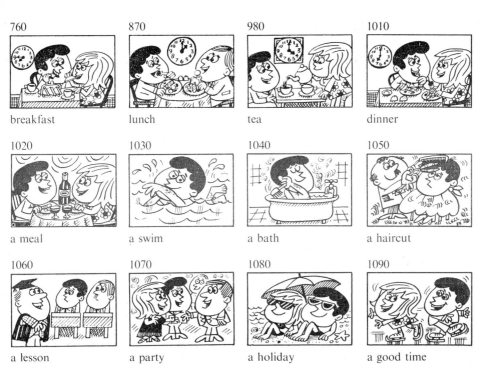

760 breakfast
870 lunch
980 tea
1010 dinner
1020 a meal
1030 a swim
1040 a bath
1050 a haircut
1060 a lesson
1070 a party
1080 a holiday
1090 a good time

Exercise

Look at this:

> I *had* a cup of coffee. I *drank* a cup of coffee.

Do these in the same way. Put in drank, enjoyed yourself, are eating, went for, ate, *or* take.
They *had* a meal at a restaurant.   They . . . a meal at a restaurant.
We *had* a holiday last month.   We . . . a holiday last month.
Have a cigarette.   . . . a cigarette.
You *had a good time*.   You . . .
They *are having* their lunch.   They . . . their lunch.
I *had* a glass of milk.   I . . . a glass of milk.

Lesson **83**

PEGGY: Húllo, Jóhn.
Cóme ín.

TOM: Húllo, Jóhn.
We're háving lúnch.
Dó you wánt to háve lúnch wíth us?
JOHN: Nó thánk you, Tóm.
I've álready hád lúnch.
Í had lúnch at hálf pást twélve.

PEGGY: Háve a cúp of cóffee then.
JOHN: Í've just hád a cup, thánk you.
I hád one áfter my lúnch.

TOM: Lét's gó into the líving-room, Péggy.
We can háve our cóffee thére.

PEGGY: Excúse the méss, Jóhn.
Thís róom's véry untídy.
We're pácking our súitcases.
We're góing to léave tomórrow.
Tóm and Í are góing to háve a hóliday.

JOHN: Áren't you lúcky!
TOM: Whén are yóu going to
háve a hóliday, Jóhn?
JOHN: I dón't knów.
I've alréady hád my hóliday thís yéar.
PEGGY: Whére did you gó?
JOHN: I stáyed at hóme!

Lesson **84**   Have you had . . . ?

1000 fruit	2000 bananas	3000 oranges	4000 peaches	5000 apples
6000 vegetables	7000 lettuce	8000 cabbage	9000 peas	10,000 beans
11,000 meat	12,000 beef	13,000 lamb	14,000 steak	15,000 chicken
16,000 milk	17,000 tea	18,000 coffee	19,000 wine	20,000 beer

Exercise
Look at this:

Have some coffee.	*I've already had some.*
Have a banana.	*I've already had one.*

Do these in the same way:
Have some beer.
Have an apple.
Have a peach.
Have some milk.
Have a glass of water.
Have a biscuit.
Have some cheese.

GEORGE: Húllo, Kén.
KEN: Húllo, Géorge.
GEORGE: Háve you just béen to the cínema?
KEN: Yés, I háve.
GEORGE: Whát's ón?
KEN: "Páris in the Spring".
GEORGE: Óh, I've alréady séen it.
         I saw it
         on a B.B.C. télevision prógramme lást yéar.
         It's an óld film,
         but it's véry góod.
KEN: Páris is a béautiful cíty.
GEORGE: I have néver béen thére.
         Have yóu ever béen there, Kén?
KEN: Yés, I háve.
         I was thére in Ápril.
GEORGE: Páris in the spríng, éh?
KEN: It was spríng,
         but the wéather was áwful.
         It ráined áll the tíme.
GEORGE: Júst líke déar óld Lóndon!

Lesson 86   What have you done?

1st
aired

2nd
cleaned

3rd
opened

4th
sharpened

5th
turned on

6th
listened to

7th
boiled

8th
answered

9th
emptied

10th
asked

11th
typed

12th
washed

13th
walked

14th
painted

15th
dusted

Exercise

Look at these two sentences:

> She has already aired the room.
> She aired it this morning.

In which of these sentences can we put has:
She . . . just boiled an egg.
She . . . boiled it a minute ago.
She . . . never been to Yugoslavia, but he . . . was there in 1966.
He . . . already painted that bookcase.
He . . . painted it a week ago.
She . . . emptied the basket this morning.
She . . . just dusted the sideboard.

Lesson **87**

MR WOOD: Ís my car réady yét?
ATTENDANT: I dón't knów, sír.
Whát's the lícence númber
of yóur cár?
MR WOOD: It's LFŹ 3í2 Ġ.
ATTENDANT: Whén did you bríng it to us?
MR WOOD: I bróught it hére thrée dáys agó.
ATTENDANT: Áh yés, I remémber now.
MR WOOD: Háve your mechánics fínished yét?
ATTENDANT: Nó, they're stíll wórking on it.
Lét's go ínto the gárage
and háve a lóok at it.

ATTENDANT: Ísn't thát yóur cár?
MR WOOD: Wéll, it *was* my car.
ATTENDANT: Dídn't your wífe have a crásh?
MR WOOD: Thát's ríght.
She dróve it into a lámp póst.
Cán your mechánics repáir it?
ATTENDANT: Wéll,
they're trýing to repáir it, sír.
But to téll you the trúth,
you néed a néw cár!

Lesson **88**   Have you . . . yet?

Have you met Mrs Jones yet?
Yes, I have.
When did you meet her?
I met her two weeks ago.

Has the boss left yet?
Yes, he has.
When did he leave?
He left ten minutes ago.

Have you had breakfast yet?
Yes, we have.
When did you have it?
We had it at half past seven.

Has she found her pen yet?
Yes, she has.
When did she find it?
She found it an hour ago.

Study these verbs:

buy	bought	bought	lose	lost	lost
find	found	found	make	made	made
get	got	got	meet	met	met
have	had	had	send	sent	sent
hear	heard	heard	sweep	swept	swept
leave	left	left	tell	told	told

Exercise

Look at this:

> He bought a house last year.
>
> QUESTION: *Did he buy a house last year?*
> NEGATIVE: *He didn't buy a house last year.*

Do these in the same way:
He found his pen a minute ago.
He got a new television last week.
We heard the news on the radio.
They left this morning.
He lost his umbrella yesterday.
I swept the floor this morning.

Lesson **89**

MR HILL: Góod afternóon.
I belíeve that
thís hóuse is for sále.
MR WEST: Thát's ríght.
MR HILL: Máy I háve a lóok at it pléase?
MR WEST: Yés, of cóurse.
Cóme ín.

MR HILL: Hów lóng have you líved hére?
MR WEST: I have líved hére for twénty yéars.
MR HILL: Twénty yéars!
Thát's a lóng tíme.
MR WEST: Yés, I have béen hére since 1947.
MR HILL: Then whý do you wánt to séll it?
MR WEST: Becáuse I have júst retíred.
I wánt to búy
a smáll hóuse in the cóuntry.
MR HILL: Hów múch does thís hóuse cóst?
MR WEST: £6850.
MR HILL: Thát's a lót of móney!
MR WEST: It's wórth évery pénny of it.
MR HILL: Wéll, I líke the hóuse,
but I cán't decíde yét.
My wífe must sée it fírst.
MR WEST: Wómen álways háve
the lást wórd.

Lesson **90**   Have you . . . yet?

1

Have you read this book yet?
Yes, I have.
When did you read it?
I read it last year.

2

Have you done your homework yet?
Yes, I have.
When did you do it?
I did it half an hour ago.

3

Has he gone yet?
Yes, he has.
When did he go?
He went an hour ago.

4

Has she spoken to him yet?
Yes, she has.
When did she speak to him?
She spoke to him yesterday.

Study these verbs:

cut	cut	cut	do	did	done	eat	ate	eaten
put	put	put	come	came	come	go	went	gone
read	read	read	give	gave	given	rise	rose	risen
set	set	set	swim	swam	swum	see	saw	seen
shut	shut	shut	take	took	taken	speak	spoke	spoken

Exercise

Look at this:

> He read this book last week.
>
> QUESTION: *Did he read this book last week?*
> NEGATIVE: *He didn't read this book last week.*

Do these in the same way:
The sun set at twenty past seven.
He ate his lunch at one o'clock.
They did their homework last night.
He came by car this morning.
The sun rose at half past five.
We swam across the river yesterday.

MRS SMITH: Hás Mr West sóld his hóuse yét?
MRS BROWN: Yés, he hás.
He sóld it lást wéek.
MRS SMITH: Hás he móved to his néw hóuse yét?
MRS BROWN: Nó, nót yét.
He's stíll hére.
He's góing to móve tomórrow.
MRS SMITH: Whén? Tomórrow mórning?
MRS BROWN: Nó. Tomórrow afternóon.
Í shall míss him.
He has álways béen a góod néighbour.
MRS GREEN: He's a véry níce pérson.
We shall áll míss him.
MRS SMITH: Whén will the néw péople
móve into this hóuse?
MRS BROWN: I thínk that they will móve ín
the dáy after tomórrow.
MRS GREEN: Wíll you sée Mr West todáy, Mrs Brówn?
MRS BROWN: Yés, I sháll.
MRS GREEN: Pléase gíve him my regárds.
MRS SMITH: Póor Mr West!
He dídn't wánt to léave this hóuse.
MRS BROWN: Nó, hé didn't wánt to léave,
but hís wife díd!

Lesson **92**

TODAY	TOMORROW	THE DAY AFTER TOMORROW
this morning	tomorrow morning	the day after tomorrow in the morning
this afternoon	tomorrow afternoon	the day after tomorrow in the afternoon
this evening	tomorrow evening	the day after tomorrow in the evening
tonight	tomorrow night	the night after next

When will . . . ?

1st
rain

2nd
snow

3rd
leave

4th
get up

5th
arrive

6th
finish work

7th
have a holiday

8th
drive home

9th
have a haircut

10th
telephone me

11th
have a shave

12th
pack his bags

13th
sweep the floor

14th
paint this room

15th
repair my car

16th
make an appointment

Exercise

Look at this:

> It *will* rain tomorrow. *It'll rain tomorrow.*

Write these again. Use short forms:
He *will* arrive tomorrow morning.
She *will* come this evening.
I *shall* see you the night after next.
We *shall* meet him next week.
It *will* snow tonight.
He *will not* believe me.
We *shall not* remain here.

Lesson **93**

Mŕ Híll is our néw néxt-dóor néighbour.
He's a pílot.

He was in the Ŕ.Á.Ḟ.

He will flý to Néw Yórk néxt mónth.

The mónth after néxt
hé will flý to Tókyo.

Át the móment,
he's in Madríd.
He fléw to Spáin a wéek agó.

He will retúrn to Lóndon
the wéek after néxt.

He's ónly fórty-óne yéars óld,
and he has alréady béen
to néarly évery cóuntry in the wórld.

Mŕ Híll is a véry lúcky mán.
But his wífe isn't véry lúcky.
She úsually stáys at hóme!

Lesson **94**

last week   this week   next week   the week after next
last month   this month   next month   the month after next
last year   this year   next year   the year after next

When did you/will you go to . . . ?

1

Accra

2

Athens

3

Berlin

4

Bombay

5

Geneva

6
London

7

Madrid

8

Moscow

9

New York

10

Paris

11

Rome

12

Stockholm

13

Sydney

14

Teheran

15

Tokyo

Exercise
Look at this:

> He went to Accra last year.
> *He will go to Accra next year.*

Do these in the same way:
He went to New York last week.
She went to Sydney last month.
I went to Paris the year before last.
We went to Stockholm last year.
They went to Geneva the week before last.

Lesson 95

GEORGE: Twó retúrn tíckets to Lóndon pléase.
What tíme will the néxt tráin léave?
ATTENDANT: At níneteen mínutes pást éight.

GEORGE: Whích plátform?
ATTENDANT: Plátform Twó.
Óver the brídge.

KEN: What tíme will the néxt tráin léave?
GEORGE: At éight netéen.
KEN: Wé've got plénty of tíme.

George: It's ónly thrée mínutes to éight.
KEN: Let's gó and háve a drínk.
Thére's a bár
néxt dóor to the státion.

GEORGE: Wé had bétter
gó báck to the státion now, Kén.

PORTER: Tíckets pléase.
GEORGE: We wánt to cátch
the éight netéen to Lóndon.
PORTER: You've júst míssed it!

GEORGE: Whát!
It's ónly éight fiftéen.
PORTER: I'm sórry, sír.
That clóck's tén mínutes slów.
GEORGE: Whén's the néxt tráin?
PORTER: In fíve hóurs' tíme!

Lesson **96** What's the exact time?

1st 2nd 3rd 4th 5th 6th

7th 8th 9th 10th 11th 12th

a minute/two minutes
an hour/two hours
a day/two days
a week/two weeks
a month/two months
a year/two years

AGO   IN

a minute's/two minutes'
an hour's/two hours'
a day's/two days'
a week's/two weeks'
a month's/two months'
a year's/two years'

TIME

When did he/will he go to . . . ?

1 Accra	2 Athens	3 Berlin	4 Bombay	5 Geneva
6 London	7 Madrid	8 Moscow	9 New York	10 Paris
11 Rome	12 Stockholm	13 Sydney	14 Teheran	15 Tokyo

Exercise
Look at this:

We must go back to the station. *We had better go back to the station.*

Change these sentences in the same way:
I must stay here.
We must wait for him.
You must call a doctor.
They must go home.
She must hurry.
You must be careful.

Lesson **97**

MR HALL:	I léft a súitcase on the tráin to Lóndon the óther dáy.	
ATTENDANT:	Cán you descríbe it, sír?	

MR HALL: It's a smáll blúe cáse
and it's gót a zíp
There's a lábel on the hándle
with my náme and addréss on it.

ATTENDANT: Ís thís cáse yóurs?
MR HALL: Nó, thát's not mine.

ATTENDANT: Whát abóut thís óne?
Thís óne's gót a lábel.
MR HALL: Lét me sée it.

ATTENDANT: Whát's your náme and addréss?
MR HALL: Dávid Háll,
8͞3, Brídge Stréet.
ATTENDANT: Thát's ríght.
Ď. Ń. Háll,
8͞3, Brídge Stréet.

ATTENDANT: Fifty·pence pléase.
MR HALL: Hére you áre.
ATTENDANT: Thánk you.

MR HALL: Héy!
ATTENDANT: Whát's the mátter?

MR HALL: Thís cáse dóesn't belóng to mé!
You've gíven me the wróng cáse!

Does this belong to me?	Is this mine?
Does this belong to you?	Is this yours?
Does this belong to him?	Is this his?
Does this belong to her?	Is this hers?
Do these belong to us?	Are these ours?
Do these belong to you?	Are these yours?
Do these belong to them?	Are these theirs?

Whose is it?
Whose are they?

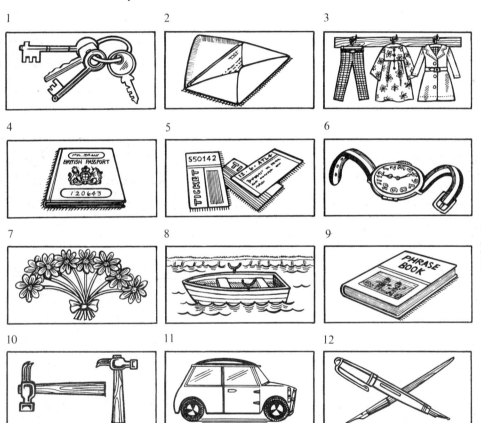

Exercise
Look at this:

This dress belongs to my sister. It *is hers.*

Do these in the same way:
These things belong to my husband. They . . .
This coat belongs to me. It . . .
These shoes belong to my wife. They . . .
These books belong to my brother and me. They . . .
These pens belong to Tom and Betty. The pens . . .
This suitcase belongs to you. It . . .

Lesson **99**

TED: Ów!

PAT: Whát's the mátter, Téd?
TED: I slípped and féll downstáirs.

PAT: Háve you húrt yoursélf?
TED: Yés, I háve.
I thínk that
I've húrt my báck.

PAT: Trý and stánd úp.
Cán you stánd úp?
Hére.
Lét me hélp you.

TED: I'm sórry, Pát.
I'm afráid that
I cán't gét úp.

PAT: I thínk that
the dóctor had bétter sée you.
I'll télephone Dŕ Cárter.

PAT: The dóctor sáys that
he will cóme at ónce.
I'm súre that
you néed an X́-ray, Téd.

Lesson **100**

| He | says
thinks
believes
knows
understands
is afraid
is sorry
is sure | **that he** | is . . .
feels . . .
has (got) . . .
needs . . .
wants . . .
can . . .
must . . .
will . . . |

He says that . . . She says that . . . They say that . . .

is/are
feel(s)

1 tired 2 thirsty 3 cold 4 ill

has/have
(got)

5 a cold 6 a headache 7 an ear-ache 8 toothache

need(s)
want(s)

9 a haircut 10 a licence 11 an X-ray 12 some money

can
must
will

13 wait 14 catch 15 repair 16 sell

Exercise

Look at this:

He is drinking his milk. *He says that he is drinking his milk.*

Do these in the same way:
She has found her pen.
They must remain here.
He remembers you.
She doesn't speak English.
They are washing the dishes.

GRANDMOTHER: Réad Jímmy's cárd to me pléase, Máry.
MARY: "I have júst arríved in Scótland
and I'm stáying at a Yóuth Hóstel."
GRANDMOTHER: Éh?
MARY: He sáys he's júst arríved in Scótland.
He sáys he's stáying at a Yóuth Hóstel.
You knów he's a mémber of the Ý.H́.Á.
GRANDMOTHER: The whát?
MARY: The Ý.H́.Á., móther.
The Yóuth Hóstels Associátion.
GRANDMOTHER: Whát élse does he sáy?
MARY: "I'll wríte a létter sóon.
I hópe you are áll wéll."
GRANDMOTHER: Whát?
Spéak úp, Máry.
I'm afráid I cán't héar you.
MARY: He sáys he'll wríte a létter sóon.
He hópes we are áll wéll.
"Lóve, Jímmy."
GRANDMOTHER: Is thát áll?
He dóesn't sáy very múch, dóes he?
MARY: He cán't wríte véry múch
on a cárd, móther.

Lesson **102**

He says thinks believes knows hopes is afraid is sorry is sure	**he** is . . . feels . . . has (got) . . . needs . . . wants . . . can . . . must . . . will . . .

He says he . . . She says she . . . They say they . . .

is/are
feel(s)

1 tired   2 thirsty   3 cold   4 ill

has/have
(got)

5 a cold   6 a headache   7 an ear ache   8 toothache

need(s)
want(s)

9 a haircut   10 a licence   11 an X-ray   12 some money

can
must
will

13 wait   14 catch   15 repair   16 sell

Exercise
Look at this:

> He is drinking his milk. *He says he has drunk his milk.*

Do these in the same way:
She is shutting the door.
He is putting on his coat.
He is reading this magazine.
They are speaking to the boss.
The sun is rising.

HARRY: Hów was the examinátion, Díck?
DICK: Nót tóo bád.
I thínk I pássed
in Énglish and Mathemátics.
The quéstions were véry éasy.
Hów abóut yóu, Hárry?
HARRY: The Énglish and Máths pápers
wéren't éasy enóugh for mé.
I hópe I háven't fáiled.
DICK: I thínk I fáiled the Intélligence Tést.
I could ánswer síxteen of the quéstions.
They were véry éasy.
But I cóuldn't ánswer the rést.
They were tóo difficult for mé.
HARRY: Intélligence tésts are áwful, áren't they?
DICK: I háte them.
I'm súre I've gót a lów Í.Q̇.
HARRY: Óh, chéer úp!
Perháps we dídn't dó tóo bádly.
The féllow néxt to mé
wróte his náme
at the tóp of the páper.
DICK: Yés?
HARRY: Then he sát thére
and lóoked at it for thrée hóurs!
He dídn't wríte a wórd!

could answer the questions.
They were very easy.
couldn't answer the questions.
They were too difficult.
The questions were easy enough for me to answer.
The questions were too difficult for me to answer.

A

easy

B

difficult

C

clever

D

stupid

cheap

F

expensive

G

fresh

H

stale

loud

J

low

K

low

L

high

soft

N

hard

O

sweet

P

sour

Exercise

Copy these sentences. Put in too, very, *or* enough.
I couldn't speak to the boss. He was . . . busy.
I couldn't go out. It was . . . cold for me to go out.
I could answer all the questions. They were . . . easy.
Is that suitcase light . . . for you to carry?
Is your brother old . . . to be a member of our association?
They couldn't see that film. They were . . . young.

Lesson **105**

THE BOSS:	Whére's Míss Símpson, Bób? I wánt her.	
BOB:	Dó you wánt to spéak to her, sír?	
THE BOSS:	Yés, I dó. I wánt her to cóme to my óffice. Téll her to cóme at ónce.	

MISS SIMPSON:	Díd you wánt to sée me, sír?	
THE BOSS:	Áh, yés, Miss Símpson. Hów do you spéll "intélligent"? Cán you téll me?	
MISS SIMPSON:	Í-Ń-T́-É-Ĺ-Ĺ-Í-Ǵ-É-Ń-T́.	

THE BOSS:	Thát's ríght. You've týped it with ónly óne "Ĺ". Thís létter's fúll of mistákes. I wánt you to týpe it agáin.	
MISS SIMPSON:	Yés, sír. I'm sórry about thát.	

THE BOSS:	And hére's a líttle présent for you.	
MISS SIMPSON:	Whát ís it?	
THE BOSS:	It's a díctionary. I hópe it will hélp you.	

K	L	M	N
carry it	correct it	listen to it	describe it
O	P	Q	R
move it	try it	finish it	keep it

don't want you to . . . Tell (him) not to . . .

S	T	U	V
hurt yourself	slip	fall	miss it
W	X	Y	Z
break it	drive it	lose it	cut yourself

Exercise

Look at this:

| Please repair it. | *I want you to repair it.* |

Do these in the same way:
Please spell it.
Please telephone him.
Please wear it.
Please ask her.
Please tell them.
Please help us.

ASSISTANT: Dó you líke thís dréss, mádam?
LADY: I líke the cólour véry múch.
It's a lóvely dréss,
but it's tóo smáll for mé.

ASSISTANT: Whát abóut thís óne?
It's a lóvely dréss.
It's véry smárt.
Shórt skírts are in fáshion nów.
Wóuld you líke to trý it?
LADY: Áll ríght.

LADY: I'm afráid thís gréen dréss
is tóo smáll for me as wéll.
It's smáller than the blúe one.

LADY: I dón't líke the cólour éither.
It dóesn't súit me at áll.
I thínk the blúe dréss is préttier.

LADY: Cóuld you shów me
anóther blúe dréss?
I wánt a dréss like thát óne,
but it múst be mý síze.

ASSISTANT: I'm afráid I háven't gót a lárger dréss.
Thís is the lárgest dréss in the shóp.

A

Alice is tall.

B

Paul is taller
than Alice.

C

Hans is the tallest
student in our class.

D

It is hot today.

E

It was hotter
yesterday.

F

The day before yesterday
was the hottest day
in the year.

G

There was a large
crowd at the race
last year.

H

This year the
crowd is larger.

I

It is the largest
crowd I have ever seen.

J

The brown suitcase
is heavy.

K
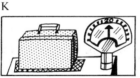
The blue suitcase
is heavier than
the brown one.

L

The green suitcase is
the heaviest of them all.

Exercise

Look at these words:

cold – colder; nice – nicer; hot – hotter; heavy – heavier.

Now look at this:

It is warm today. but it was . . . yesterday.
It is warm today, but it was warmer yesterday.

Do these in the same way:
It is cool today, but it was . . . yesterday.
It is wet today, but it was . . . yesterday.
He's late again today, but he was . . . yesterday.
This test is easy, but that one is . . .
This bookcase is large, but that one is . . .
Betty is pretty, but Jane is . . .

BETTY: Sháll I máke some cóffee, Jáne?
JANE: Thát's a góod idéa, Bétty.

BETTY: It's réady.
Dó you wánt any mílk?
JANE: Júst a líttle pléase.

BETTY: Whát abóut some súgar?
Twó téaspoonfúls?
JANE: Nó, léss than thát.
Óne and a hálf téaspoonfúls pléase.
Thát's enóugh for mé.

JANE: Thát was véry níce.
BETTY: Wóuld you líke some móre?
JANE: Yés, pléase.

JANE: I'd líke a cigarétte, tóo.
Máy I háve óne?
BETTY: Of cóurse.
I thínk there are a féw in thát bóx.

JANE: I'm afráid it's émpty.
BETTY: Whát a píty!
JANE: It dóesn't mátter.

BETTY: Háve a bíscuit instéad.
Éat móre and smóke léss!
JANE: Thát's véry góod àdvíce!

ave you got any chocolate?
haven't got much.

J

I've got more than you have.

K

I've got the most.

ave you got any chocolate?
ve got very little.

M

I've got less than you have.

N

I've got the least.

ave you made any mistakes?
haven't made many.

P

I've made more than you
have.

Q

I've made the most.

ave you made any mistakes?
e made very few.

S

I've made fewer than you
have.

T

I've made the fewest.

ou must see my new car.
s very good.

V

This one's better.

W

This one's the best
I've ever seen.

ou mustn't go to
at restaurant.
s very bad.

Y

This one's worse.

Z

This one's the worst
I've ever seen.

xercise

py these sentences. Put in much, many, less *or* fewer.
aven't got any cigarettes. I haven't got . . . either.
e got some money. I've got . . . than you have.
aven't got any money. I haven't got . . . either.
e got some books. I've got . . . than you have.

Lesson **111**

MR FRITH: I líke this récord-pláyer véry múch.
Hów múch does it cóst pléase?
ASSISTANT: It's the móst expénsive módel
in the shóp.
It cósts síxty-fóur póunds.

MRS FRITH: That's tóo expénsive for ús.
We cán't affórd áll thát móney.

ASSISTANT: Thís módel's léss expénsive
than thát óne.
It's ónly twénty-éight póunds.
But, of cóurse,
it's nót as góod as the expénsive óne.

MR FRITH: I dón't líke thís módel.
The óther módel's móre expénsive,
but it's wórth the móney.

MR FRITH: Cán we búy it on instálments?
ASSISTANT: Of cóurse.
You can páy a depósit of tén póunds,
and then óne póund a wéek
for síxty wéeks.

MR FRITH: Dó you líke it, déar?
MRS FRITH: I cértainly dó,
but I dón't líke the príce.
You álways wánt the bést,
but we cán't affórd it.
Sómetimes you thínk
you're a míllionáire!
MR FRITH: Míllionáires dón't búy thíngs
on instálments!

Lesson 112 How do they compare?

As . . . as

a   b   c  d   e   f

sweet   tall   short   old   blunt   sharp

Not as . . . as

g   h   i   j   k   l

clean   fat   smart   light   new   expensive

m

This test is difficult.

n

This test is more difficult.

o

This is the most difficult test I have ever done!

p

This book is interesting.

q

This book is less interesting.

r

This is the least interesting book I have ever read!

Exercise

Look at these sentences:

> This dress is long, but that one is . . .
> *This dress is long, but that one is longer.*
> Tom is intelligent, but Bill is . . .
> *Tom is intelligent, but Bill is more intelligent.*

Do these in the same way:
This book is cheap, but that one is . . .
This book is expensive, but that one is . . .
This question is easy, but that one is . . .
This question is difficult, but that one is . . .
Miss Jones is pretty, but Miss Brown is . . .
Miss Green is beautiful, but Miss White is . . .

Lesson **113**

CONDUCTOR:	Făres pléase!
MAN:	Trafálgar Squáre pléase.
CONDUCTOR:	I'm sórry, sír.
	I cán't chánge a póund nóte.
	Háven't you gót
	any smáll chánge?
MAN:	I've gót no smáll chánge,
	I'm afráid.
CONDUCTOR:	I'll ásk sóme of the pássengers.

CONDUCTOR:	Háve you ány smáll chánge, sír?
1st PASSENGER:	I'm sórry.
	I've gót none.
2nd PASSENGER:	Í háven't gót any éither.

CONDUCTOR:	Cán you chánge
	thís póund nóte, mádam?
3rd PASSENGER:	I'm afráid I cán't.
4th PASSENGER:	Néither can Í.

CONDUCTOR:	I'm véry sórry, sír.
	You must gét óff the bús.
	Nóne of our pássengers
	can chánge thís nóte.
	They're áll míllionáires!

TWO TRAMPS:	Excépt ús, condúctor.
1st TRAMP:	Í've got some smáll chánge.
2nd TRAMP:	Só have Í.

Lesson **114**   I've got none

o

Have you got any
chocolate?

p

I haven't got any.
I've got no chocolate.
I've got none.

q

I haven't any either.
Neither have I.

r

Have you got any
envelopes?

s

I haven't got any.
I've got no envelopes.
I've got none.

t

I haven't any either.
Neither have I.

u

Have you got any
cake?

v

I've got some.

w

So have I.

x

Have you got any
biscuits?

y

I've got some.

z

So have I.

Exercise
Look at this:

There isn't any milk in that bottle. *There is no milk in that bottle.*

Change these sentences in the same way:
There aren't any books on that shelf.
I haven't got any money.
There isn't any coffee in this tin.
I didn't see any cars in the street.
I haven't got any envelopes.

HELEN: Ísn't there ányone at hóme?
JIM: I'll knóck agáin, Hélen.
Éverything's véry quíet.
I'm súre there's nó one at hóme.

HELEN: But thát's impóssible.
Pát and Tóm invíted us to lúnch.
Lóok through the wíndow.

HELEN: Cán you sée ánything?
JIM: Nóthing at áll.

HELEN: Lét's trý the báck dóor.
JIM: Lóok! Éveryone's in the gárden.

PAT: Húllo, Hélen. Húllo, Jím.
TOM: Éverybody wánts to háve lúnch
in the gárden.
It's níce and wárm out hére.

PAT: Cóme and háve sómething to drínk.
JIM: Thánks, Pát.
Máy I háve a gláss of béer pléase?
PAT: Béer?
There's nóne léft.
You can háve some lemonáde.
JIM: Lémonáde!

TOM: Dón't belíeve her, Jím.
She's ónly jóking.
Háve some béer!

Lesson 116   Every, No, Any and Some

Every	None	Any	Some
Everyone	No one	Anyone	Someone
Everybody	Nobody	Anybody	Somebody
Everything	Nothing	Anything	Something
Everywhere	Nowhere	Anywhere	Somewhere

a

Everyone is asleep.
Everybody is asleep.

b

Everything is untidy.

c

I looked for my pen
everywhere.

d

Is there anyone
at home?
Is there anybody at home?

e

Is there anything
in that box?

f

I couldn't find my
pen anywhere.

g

There's no one
at home.
There's nobody
at home.

h

There's nothing
in this box.

i

Where did you go
yesterday?
Nowhere. I stayed
at home.

j

There's someone
in the garden.
There's somebody
in the garden.

k

There's something
under that chair!

l

My glasses must be
somewhere!
You're wearing them!

Exercise
Look at this:

> I didn't buy *anything*. *I bought nothing.*

Change these in the same way:
I didn't do *anything*.
I didn't see *anyone*.
I didn't go *anywhere*.
I didn't meet *anybody*.

118

Whén my húsband was góing
into the díning-róom this mórning,
he drópped some cóins on the flóor.

Thére wére cóins éverywhere.
We lóoked for them,
but we cóuld not fínd them all.

Whíle we were háving bréakfast,
our líttle bóy, Tómmy,
fóund twó smáll cóins on the flóor.

He pút them bóth into his móuth.
We bóth tríed to gét the cóins,
but it was tóo láte.
Tómmy had alréady swállowed them!

Láter that mórning,
when I was dóing the hóusework,
my húsband télephoned me
from the óffice.

"Hów's Tómmy?" he ásked.
"I dón't knów," I ánswered,
"Tómmy's béen to the lávatory
thrée tímes thís mórning,
but I háven't hád any chánge yét!"

Someone knocked at the door
when I was having breakfast.

When I was leaving the house,
the postman arrived.

Just as I was opening the
front door, the telephone rang.

She slipped and hurt herself
while she was getting off the bus.

He cut himself
while he was shaving.

My wife was cooking the dinner,
while I was working in the garden.

Exercise

Look at this:

He arrived. I had a bath. *He arrived when I was having a bath.*

Join these sentences in the same way. Use when.
He knocked at the door. I answered the telephone.
He came downstairs. I had breakfast.
The telephone rang. I washed the dishes.
The boss arrived. She typed a letter.
The train left. I bought the tickets.
It rained heavily. I drove to London.

Dó you líke stóries?
I wánt to téll you a trúe story.
It háppened to a fríend of míne a yéar agó.

Whíle my fríend, Géorge, was réading in béd,
twó thíeves clímbed into his kítchen.

Áfter they had éntered the hóuse,
they wént into the díning-róom.
It was véry dárk,
so they túrned on a tórch.

Súddenly, they héard a vóice behínd them.
"Whát's úp? Whát's úp?" sómeone cálled.
The thíeves drópped the tórch
and rán awáy as quíckly as they cóuld.

Géorge héard the nóise
and cáme dównstáirs quíckly.

He túrned on the líght,
but he cóuldn't sée ányone.
The thíeves had alréady góne.

But Géorge's párrot, Hénry, was stíll thére.
"Whát's úp, Géorge?" he cálled.
"Nóthing, Hénry," Géorge sáid and smíled.
"Gó back to sléep."

I asked the price of the car,
but they had already sold it.

t

I ran to the platform quickly,
but the train had already left.

He gave us our copybooks
after he had corrected them.

v

She went on holiday
after she had taken the examination.

She had finished the housework
before she went out.

x

We had had dinner
before they arrived.

Exercise

Look at this:

> She went home. She typed the letter.
> *She went home after she had typed the letter.*

Join these sentences in the same way. Use after.

He dropped the vase. He took it into the living-room.
He bought another car. He sold his old one.
She swept the floor. She dusted everything.
She drank the milk. She boiled it.
He turned off the television. He saw the programme.
He went to bed. He did his homework.

CUSTOMER:	Í bóught twó expénsive díctionaries here hálf an hóur agó, but I forgót to táke them wíth me.

MANAGER:	Whó sérved you, sír?
CUSTOMER:	The lády who is stánding behínd the cóunter.

MANAGER:	Whích bóoks did you búy?
CUSTOMER:	The bóoks which are ón the cóunter.

MANAGER:	Díd you sérve thís géntleman hálf an hóur agó, Miss Róberts? He sáys he's the mán who bóught thése bóoks.
MISS ROBERTS:	I cán't remémber, sír. The mán whom Í sérved was wéaring a hát.

MANAGER:	Háve you gót a hát, sír?
CUSTOMER:	Yés, I háve.
MANAGER:	Wóuld you pút it ón, pléase?
CUSTOMER:	Áll ríght.

MANAGER:	Is thís the mán that you sérved, Miss Róberts?
MISS ROBERTS:	Yés, sír. I récognize him nów.

1

Who served you?
The man who/that is
standing behind the
counter.

2

Who served you?
The woman who/that is
standing behind the
counter.

3

Who is making all
that noise?
The men who/that are
repairing the road.

4

I served him
yesterday.
He is the man whom/
that I served
yesterday.

5

I served her
yesterday.
She is the woman
whom/that I served
yesterday.

6

I saw them
yesterday.
They are the men
whom/that I saw
yesterday.

7

Which book did
you buy?
The book which/that
is on the counter.

8

Which books did
you buy?
The books which/that
are on the counter.

9

Which dog is yours?
The dog which/that
is carrying that
basket.

Exercise

Look at these sentences:

> She is the girl. *She* met me yesterday.
> She is the girl *who* met me yesterday.
>
> She is the girl. I met *her* yesterday.
> She is the girl *whom* I met yesterday.
>
> This is the book. I bought *it* yesterday.
> This is the book *which* I bought yesterday.

Join these sentences in the same way. Use who, whom *or* which.
This is the car. The mechanic repaired *it* yesterday.
He is the man. I invited *him* to the party.
These are the things. I bought *them* yesterday.
He is the man. *He* came here last week.
He is the policeman. *He* caught the thieves.
She is the nurse. *She* looked after me.
She is the woman. I met *her* at the party.
I am the person. *I* wrote to you.

BILL: Lóok, Bób.
This is a phótograph I took
dúring my tríp to Austrália.
BOB: Lét me sée it, Bíll.

BOB: Thís is a góod phótograph.
Whó are thése péople?
BILL: They're péople I mét dúring the tríp.

BILL: Thát's the shíp
we trávelled on.
BOB: What a béautiful shíp!

BOB: Whó's thís?
BILL: Thát's the mán I tóld you abóut.
Remémber?
BOB: Áh yés.
The óne who óffered you
a jób in Austrália.
BILL: Thát's ríght.

BOB: Whó's thís?
BILL: Guéss!
BOB: It's nót yóu, ís it?
BILL: Thát's ríght.

BILL: I gréw a béard dúring the tríp,
but I sháved it óff
whén I cáme hóme.
BOB: Whý did you sháve it óff?
BILL: My wífe dídn't líke it!

Lesson **124** (Who)/(Whom), (Which) and (That)

1

Who served you?
The man standing
behind the counter.

2

Who served you?
The woman standing
behind the counter.

3

Who is making all
that noise?
The men repairing the road.

4

I served him
yesterday.
He is the man
I served yesterday.

5

I served her
yesterday.
She is the woman
I served yesterday.

6

I saw them
yesterday.
They are the men
I saw yesterday.

7

What's this?
This is the book
I bought yesterday.

8

What are these?
These are the books
I bought yesterday.

9

What's this?
This is the kitten
I found in the garden.

Exercise

Look at these sentences:

> She is the girl. I met *her* yesterday.
> She is the girl I met yesterday.
>
> This is the book. I bought *it* yesterday.
> This is the book I bought yesterday.
>
> This is the ship. I travelled on *it*.
> This is the ship I travelled on.

Join these sentences in the same way:
She is the woman. I drove *her* to London.
That's the film. I saw *it*.
That's the man. I spoke to *him*.
They are the thieves. The police caught *them*.
These are the letters. I typed *them*.
These are the people. You asked me about *them*.
These are the shoes. The boy took *them* off.

SUSAN: Cán't you cóme ín
and háve téa nów, Péter?
PETER: Nót yét, déar.
I must wáter the gárden fírst.

SUSAN: Do you háve to wáter it nów?
PETER: I'm afráid I múst.
Lóok at it!
It's térribly drý.

SUSAN: Whát a núisance!
PETER: Lást summer it was véry drý, tóo.
Dón't you remémber?
I had to wáter it évery dáy.
SUSAN: Wéll, I'll háve téa by mysélf.

SUSAN: Thát was quíck!
Háve you fínished alréady?
PETER: Yés, déar.
Lóok out of the wíndow.

SUSAN: Góod héavens!
It's ráining.
Thát méans
you néedn't wáter the gárden.
PETER: That was a pléasant surpríse.
It méans I can háve téa, instéad.

Lesson **126** Must, Have to and Needn't

1

Must you go now?
Yes, I have to leave
immediately.

2

Must you get up early tomorrow
morning?
Yes, I shall have to get up
at six o'clock.

3

Did you have to take a taxi?
I'm afraid I had to.
I couldn't get a bus.

4

Hasn't your girl friend arrived
yet? How long have you had to wait?
I have had to wait for two hours!

5

Must you water the garden?
No, I needn't water it now.
It's going to rain.

6

Do we have to walk to the station?
No, we needn't.
We can catch a bus.

Exercise

Look at these sentences:

> You have to leave early.
> Do you have to leave early?
> You don't have to leave early.
>
> She must leave early.
> Must she leave early?
> She needn't leave early.

Copy each of these sentences. Then write a question and a negative:
She has to decide immediately.
She must decide immediately.
We have to take a taxi.
We must take a taxi.

KATE: Cán you récognize thát wóman, Míllie?
MILLIE: I thínk I cán, Káte.
It múst be Káren Mársh, the áctress.
KATE: I thóught só.
Whó's thát besíde her?
MILLIE: Thát must be Cónrad Réeves.
KATE: Cónrad Réeves, the áctor?
It cán't be.
Lét me háve anóther lóok.
I thínk you're ríght!
Ísn't he her thírd húsband?
MILLIE: Nó. He múst be her fóurth or fífth.
KATE: Dóesn't Káren Mársh lóok óld!
MILLIE: She dóes, dóesn't she!
I réad she's twénty-níne,
but she múst be at léast fórty.
KATE: I'm súre she ís.
MILLIE: Shé was a fámous áctress
when Í was stíll a schóolgirl.
KATE: Thát was a lóng tíme agó, wásn't it?
MILLIE: Not *thát* long agó!
Í'm not móre than twénty-níne mysélf.

He can't be ill.
He must be tired.

2

It can't be my new hat.
It must be my old one.

She can't be Danish.
She must be Swedish.

4

He can't be a dentist.
He must be a doctor.

She can't be forty.
She must be fifty.

6

It can't be the 20th.
It must be the 21st.

He can't be the youngest.
He must be the oldest.

8

He can't be reading.
He must be sleeping.

Exercise

Look at these sentences:

He must be home before six o'clock.
He has to be home before six o'clock.
He must be tired.

In which of these sentences can we put has to *instead of* must:
He must be here at six o'clock.
He must be busy.
He must be at the office early tomorrow.
He must be sleeping.
He must be French.
He must be in France next week.
He must be an engineer.

ANN:	Lóok, Hárry! Thát políceman's wáving to you. He wánts you to stóp.	 1
POLICEMAN: HARRY: POLICEMAN:	Whére do you thínk you áre? Ón a ráce tráck? You múst have been dríving at séventy míles an hóur. I cán't have béen. Í was dóing éighty whén I óvertóok you.	 2
POLICEMAN: HARRY: ANN: HARRY:	Dídn't you sée the spéed límit? I'm afráid I dídn't, ófficer. I múst have been dréaming. He wásn't dréaming, ófficer. Í was télling him to dríve slówly. Thát's why I dídn't sée the sígn.	 3
POLICEMAN:	Lét me sée your dríving-lícence and your insúrance certíficate.	 4
POLICEMAN: HARRY:	I wón't chárge you thís tíme. But you'd bétter nót dó it agáin! Thánk you. I'll cértainly bé móre cáreful.	 5
ANN: HARRY: ANN:	I tóld you to dríve slówly, Hárry. You álways téll me to dríve slówly, déar. Well, néxt tíme you'd bétter táke my advíce!	 6

He can't have been . . .
            He must have been . . .

1

He can't have been ill.
He must have been tired.

2

It can't have been my new hat.
It must have been my old one.

3

She can't have been Danish.
She must have been Swedish.

4

He can't have been a dentist.
He must have been a doctor.

5

She can't have been forty.
She must have been fifty.

6

It can't have been the 20th.
It must have been the 21st.

7

He can't have been the youngest.
He must have been the oldest.

8

He can't have been reading.
He must have been sleeping.

Exercise

Look at these sentences:

> He is very tired because he *had to* get up early this morning.
> He didn't get up early this morning. He *must have been* tired.

Copy these sentences. Put in had to *or* must have been.
He didn't come to work yesterday. He . . . ill.
He didn't come to the office this morning. He . . . stay at home.
I don't think she was Austrian. She . . . German.
I lost my pen so I . . . buy a new one.
He forgot his case so he . . . return home.
She didn't hear the telephone. She . . . sleeping.

ROY: Whére are you góing to
         spénd your hólidays thís yéar, Hárry?
HARRY: We máy gó abróad.
         I'm nót súre.
         My wífe wánts to gó to Égypt.
         Í'd líke to gó there, tóo.
         We cán't máke úp óur mínds.
ROY: Wíll you trável by séa or by áir?
HARRY: We máy trável by séa.
ROY: It's chéaper, ísn't it?
HARRY: It máy be chéaper,
         but it tákes a lóng tíme.
ROY: I'm súre you will enjóy yóursélves.
HARRY: Dón't bé só súre.
         We máy nót gó ánywhere.
         My wífe álways wórries tóo múch.
         Whó's góing to lóok áfter the dóg?
         Whó's góing to lóok áfter the hóuse?
         Whó's góing to lóok áfter the gárden?
         We háve thís próblem évery yéar.
         Ín the énd, we stáy at hóme
         and lóok áfter éverything!

He may be . . .
He may have been . . .
I'm not sure

Where's Harry?
He may be in his room.
I'm not sure.

2

Where will he go?
He may go to the cinema.
I'm not sure.

Why is he late?
He may be busy.
I'm not sure.

4

What is he doing?
He may be reading.
I'm not sure.

Why was he late?
He may have been busy.
I'm not sure.

6

What was he doing?
He may have been reading.
I'm not sure.

Exercise

Read the conversation in Lesson 131 *again. Then write answers to these questions:*

Is Roy talking to Harry?
Where may Harry and his wife go this year?
Who wants to go to Egypt?
How will they travel?
Isn't it cheaper to travel by sea?
Doesn't it take a long time?
Why may Harry and his wife not go anywhere?

REPORTER: Háve you júst máde
a néw fílm, Míss Mársh?
MISS MARSH: Yés, I háve.
REPORTER: Áre you góing to máke anóther?
MISS MARSH: Nó, I'm nót.
I'm góing to retíre.
I féel véry tíred.
I dón't wánt to máke anóther fílm
for a lóng tíme.

KATE: Lét's búy a néwspaper, Míllie.
Lísten to thís!
"Káren Mársh: Sensátional Néws!
by our repórter, Álan Jones.
Míss Káren Mársh arríved
at Lóndon Áirport todáy.
She was wéaring a blúe dréss
and a mínk cóat.
She tóld me
she had júst máde a néw fílm.
She sáid
she was nót góing to máke anóther.
She sáid she was góing to rétire.
She tóld repórters she félt véry tíred
and dídn't wánt to máke
anóther fílm for a lóng tíme."
MILLIE: Wéll, fáncy thát, Káte!

1 'm tired.

2

What did he say?
What did he tell you?

3

He said (that) he was tired.
He told me (that) he was
tired.

4 'm reading.

5

What did she say?
What did she tell you?

6

She said (that) she was
reading.
She told me (that) she
was reading.

7 We want our dinner.

8

What did they say?
What did they tell you?

9

They said (that) they
wanted their dinner.
They told me (that)
they wanted their dinner.

10 've finished my homework.

11

What did he say?
What did he tell you?

12

He said (that) he had
finished his homework.
He told me (that) he had
finished his homework.

Exercise

Read the conversation in Lesson 133 again. Then write answers to these questions:

1 Has Miss Marsh just made a new film?
2 Who was asking her questions?
3 What is Miss Marsh going to do?
4 Why doesn't Miss Marsh want to make another film?
5 Who bought a newspaper?
6 Where did Miss Marsh arrive?
7 What was Miss Marsh wearing?

REPORTER: Áre you réally
góing to retíre, Míss Mársh?
MISS MARSH: I máy.
I cán't máke úp my mínd.
I shall háve to ásk
my fúture húsband.
He won't lét me máke anóther fílm.

REPORTER: Your fúture húsband, Míss Mársh?
MISS MARSH: Yés. Lét me introdúce him to you.
His náme is Cárlos.
We shall gét márried néxt wéek.

KATE: Lóok, Míllie!
Hére's anóther repórt about
Káren Mársh.
Lísten: "Káren Mársh: The Látest.
At her Lóndon Hotél todáy
Míss Mársh tóld repórters
she míght retíre.
She sáid she cóuldn't
máke úp her mínd.
She sáid she wóuld háve to
ásk her fúture húsband.
She sáid her fúture húsband
wóuld not lét her
máke anóther fílm.
Thén she introdúced us to Cárlos
and tóld us
they wóuld gét márried néxt wéek."

MILLIE: Thát's sensátional néws, ísn't it,
Káte?
KATE: It cértainly ís.
Hé'll be her síxth húsband!

He said (that) he . . .
He told me (that) he . . .

1

I shall leave
tomorrow.

2

What did he say?
What did he tell you?

3

He said (that) he would
leave tomorrow.
He told me (that) he
would leave tomorrow.

4

I can't do this
Maths problem.

5

What did he say?
What did he tell you?

6

He said (that) he couldn't
do this Maths problem.
He told me (that) he
couldn't do this Maths
problem.

7

I may return at
six o'clock.

8

What did she say?
What did she tell you?

9

She said (that) she might
return at six o'clock.
She told me (that) she
might return at six
o'clock.

Exercise

Read the conversation in Lesson 135 *again. Then write answers to these questions:*
1   Is Miss Marsh really going to retire, or is she still not sure?
2   She can't make up her mind, can she?
3   What is the name of her future husband?
4   When will they get married?
5   Where is Miss Marsh staying?
6   Did Miss Marsh introduce Carlos to the reporters?
7   How did Millie describe the news?

JUNE: Áre you dóing the fóotball póols, Brían?

BRIAN: Yés, I've néarly fínished, Júne.
I'm súre we shall wín sómething thís wéek.

JUNE: You álways sáy thát,
but we néver wín ánything!
Whát will you dó
if you wín a lót of móney?

BRIAN: Íf I wín a lót of móney
I shall búy you a mínk cóat.

JUNE: Í dón't wánt a mínk cóat!
Í want to sée the wórld.

BRIAN: Áll ríght.
Íf we wín a lót of móney
we shall trável róund the wórld
and we shall stáy at the bést hotéls.
Thén we shall retúrn hóme
and búy a bíg hóuse in the cóuntry.
We shall háve a béautiful gárden and . . .

JUNE: But íf we spénd áll thát móney
we shall be póor agáin.
Whát shall we dó thén?

BRIAN: Íf we spénd all the móney
we shall trý and wín the fóotball póols agáin.

JUNE: It's a pléasant dréam
but éverything depénds on "íf"!

Lesson **138**   If . . .

1

If you break this window,
you will have to pay for it!

2

If you don't hurry,
we shall miss the train.

3

If he falls,   .
he will hurt himself.

4

If it rains tomorrow,
we shan't go to the seaside.

5

If you feel better,
you can get up.

6

If he sells that car,
he can buy a new one.

Exercise

Read the conversation in Lesson 137 again. Then write answers to these questions:
1   What is Brian doing?
2   Has Brian ever won anything on the football pools?
3   What will Brian buy his wife if he wins a lot of money?
4   She doesn't want a mink coat, does she?
5   What does June want instead of a mink coat?
6   What will Brian do if he spends all the money?
7   It's only a dream, isn't it?
8   What does it all depend on?

MR GRIMES: Ís thát yóu, Jóhn?
JOHN SMITH: Yés, spéaking.
MR GRIMES: Téll Máry we shall be láte
for dínner this évening.
JOHN SMITH: I'm afráid I dón't understánd.
MR GRIMES: Hásn't Máry tóld you?
She invíted Bétty and mé
to dínner this évening.
I sáid I would bé
at yóur hóuse at síx o'clóck,
but the bóss wánts me
to dó some éxtra wórk.
I'll háve to stáy at the óffice.
I dón't knów whén I shall fínish.
Óh, and bý the wáy,
Mý wífe wánts to knów
if Máry néeds ány hélp.
JOHN SMITH: I dón't knów whát you're tálking abóut.
MR GRIMES: That ís Jóhn Smíth, ísn't it?
JOHN SMITH: Yés, Í'm Jóhn Smíth.
MR GRIMES: You áre Jóhn Smíth, the enginéer, áren't you?
JOHN SMITH: Thát's ríght.
MR GRIMES: You wórk
for the Óverséas Enginéering Cómpany, dón't you?
JOHN SMITH: Nó, I dón't.
I'm Jóhn Smíth the télephone enginéer
and I'm repáiring your télephone líne.

1

Are you tired?

Why are you tired?

2

What does he want
to know?
What does he want
to know?

3

He wants to know
if you are tired.
He wants to know
why you are tired.

4

Are you reading?

What are you
reading?

5

What does he want
to know?
What does he want
to know?

6

He wants to know
if you are reading.
He wants to know
what you are reading.

7

Does Tom always do
his homework?

When does Tom do his
homework?

8

What does he want
to know?

What does he want
to know?

9

He wants to know if
Tom always does his
homework.
He wants to know when
Tom does his homework.

Exercise

Read the conversation in Lesson 139 again. Then write answers to these questions:
1   Isn't Mr Grimes speaking to John Smith?
2   Who invited Mr and Mrs Grimes to dinner?
3   What time did Mr Grimes say he would be there?
4   Why can't he be there at six o'clock?
5   Mr Grimes doesn't know when he will finish work, does he?
6   What does Mr Grimes' wife want to know?
7   What's John Smith's job?
8   What is John Smith doing?

Lást wéek, my fóur yéar óld dáughter, Sálly,
was invíted to a chíldren's párty.
I decíded to táke her by tráin.
Sálly was véry excíted
becáuse she had néver trávelled
on a tráin befóre.
She sát near the wíndow
and ásked quéstions
about éverything she sáw.
Súddenly, a míddle-áged lády
cáme into óur compártment
and sát ópposite Sálly.
"Húllo, líttle gírl," she sáid.
Sálly did not ánswer,
but lóoked at her cúriously.
The lády was dréssed in a blúe cóat
and a lárge, fúnny hát.
Áfter the tráin had léft the státion,
the lády ópened her hándbag
and tóok out· her pówder cómpact.
She thén begán to máke up her fáce.
"Whý are you dóing thát?" Sálly ásked.
"To máke myself béautiful," the lády ánswered.
She pút awáy her cómpact and smíled kíndly.
"But you are stíll úgly," Sally sáid.
Sálly was amúsed,
but Í was véry embárrassed!

Lesson **142** Someone invited Sally to a party
Sally was invited to a party

1

She is embarrassed.

2

They are worried.

3

Does anyone ever repair
this car?

4

Someone repairs it regularly.
It is repaired regularly.

5

Does anyone ever correct
these copybooks?

6

Someone corrects them regularly.
They are corrected regularly.

7

Did anyone meet him at the
station this morning?

8

Someone met him at the station
this morning.
He was met at the station this
morning.

Exercise

Read the story in Lesson 141 again. Then write answers to these questions:
1 How old is Sally?
2 Why did Sally's mother decide to take her by train?
3 Where did Sally sit?
4 Who came into the compartment?
5 How was the lady dressed?
6 What did the lady do?
7 Why did the lady make up her face?
8 Did Sally think the lady was beautiful?

Í líve in a véry óld tówn
which is surróunded by béautiful wóods.
It is a fámous béauty spót.
On Súndays, húndreds of péople
cóme from the cíty
to sée óur tówn
and to wálk through the wóods.
Vísitors have been ásked
to kéep the wóods cléan and tídy.
Lítter-báskets have been pláced únder the trées,
but péople stíll thrów their rúbbish éverywhere.
Lást Wédnesday, I wént for a wálk in the wóods.
Whát I sáw
máde me véry sád.
I cóunted séven óld cárs
and thrée óld refrígerators.
The lítter-báskets were émpty
and the gróund was cóvered with
píeces of páper, cigarétte-énds, óld týres,
émpty bóttles and rústy tíns.
Amóng the rúbbish
I fóund a sígn which sáid:
"Ányone who léaves lítter in thése wóods
will be prósecuted."!

Lesson **144**   He hasn't been served yet
He will be served soon

1

Hasn't anyone repaired this car yet?

2

It has already been repaired!

3

Hasn't anyone corrected
these copybooks yet?

4

They have already been corrected!

5

Hasn't anyone caught the
thief yet?

6

He hasn't been caught yet.
He will be caught soon!

7

Hasn't anyone caught the
thieves yet?

8

They haven't been caught yet.
They will be caught soon!

Exercise

Read the piece in Lesson 143 *again. Then write answers to these questions:*
1   Where does the writer live?
2   Why do visitors often come from the city?
3   What have visitors been asked to do?
4   Where have litter-baskets been placed?
5   Where did the writer go last Wednesday?
6   He saw a lot of rubbish, didn't he?
7   What did he see among the rubbish?
8   What did the sign say?

MASK

Cut along the dotted
line.

This is the correct shape
for the mask. If you
would like to make your
own, you can cut it out
of stiffer paper.

MASK

Cut along the dotted
line.

This is the correct shape
for the mask. If you
would like to make your
own, you can cut it out
of stiffer paper.